英語 Make Me High 系列

108課綱、各類英檢考試 適用

Cloze & Writing Practice

克漏字
與寫作練習

附解析本

李文玲　編著

三民書局

國家圖書館出版品預行編目資料

Cloze & Writing Practice 克漏字與寫作練習／李文玲
編著.――修訂三版四刷.――臺北市：三民，2021
　　面；　公分.――（英語Make Me High系列）

　　ISBN 978-957-14-5969-1 （平裝）
　　1. 英語教學 2. 讀本 3. 寫作法 4. 中等教育

524.38　　　　　　　　　　　　　　103021753

Cloze & Writing Practice 克漏字與寫作練習

編 著 者	李文玲
發 行 人	劉振強
出 版 者	三民書局股份有限公司
地　　址	臺北市復興北路 386 號 (復北門市)
	臺北市重慶南路一段 61 號 (重南門市)
電　　話	(02)25006600
網　　址	三民網路書店 https://www.sanmin.com.tw
出版日期	初版一刷 2001 年 10 月
	修訂三版一刷 2016 年 2 月
	修訂三版四刷 2021 年 12 月
書籍編號	S803980
I S B N	978-957-14-5969-1

三民書局

序

英語 Make Me High 系列的理想在於超越，在於創新。

這是時代的精神，也是我們出版的動力；

這是教育的目的，也是我們進步的執著。

針對英語的全球化與未來的升學趨勢，

我們設計了一系列適合普高、技高學生的英語學習書籍。

面對英語，不會徬徨不再迷惘，學習的心徹底沸騰，

心情好 High！

實戰模擬，掌握先機知己知彼，百戰不殆決勝未來，

分數更 High！

選擇優質的英語學習書籍，才能激發學習的強烈動機；

興趣盎然便不會畏懼艱難，自信心要自己大聲說出來。

本書如良師指引循循善誘，如益友相互鼓勵攜手成長。

展書輕閱，你將發現……

學習英語原來也可以這麼 High！

給讀者的話

一、本書特點：

「克漏字與寫作練習」此書的設計是運用三十篇短文，將「克漏字」與「寫作」兩大重要題型充分的結合，讓您可以同時加強「文法句型概念」及「寫作技巧」。

本書以結合「閱讀」和「寫作」的學習為設計目標。各單元短文本身就是很好的範文，配合翻譯與短文解析，讓您在閱讀中學習寫作。本書所選之短文題材內容多元廣泛，您可以從輕鬆有趣的文章中複習學過的基礎句式結構，並進而從中循序漸進地學習寫作概念及技巧。

本書出版至今，感謝各位讀者的支持與指教。為了提供更完整的寫作練習，並配合大考測驗的趨勢，此次全新改版在原有的設計架構上再新增十個單元，提供您更多的練習機會。同時調整寫作部分的架構，在增加的篇幅中補充更完整的解說及多元的寫作活動。

二、本書架構：

Unit 1–18 (Basic)

1. 短文之後附上依文章內容設計的「問答題」，讓您練習以完整的句子回答，句數不限，如有興趣也可以延伸為 essay questions 的練習。

2. 「句式分析」的內容除短文中出現過的句型之外，另外再視情況補充額外的重要句型，並附上大量的例句供您模仿學習。

3. 「造句」、「合併或改寫句子」及「翻譯」題型讓您練習前面所學過的重要句型和片語。

Unit 19–30 (Advanced)

1. 寫作要點：

　　介紹如何寫段落、摘要、書信及短文。另外在 Unit 26–29 中的「短文解析」，特別介紹短文中的寫作技巧。

2. 寫作練習：

　　依照單元主題設計不同性質或文體的寫作練習（包括配合學測作文設計的看圖寫作練習），從「引導」到「自由發揮」，循序漸進地引導您練習寫作。每個單元並都附有一篇參考範例讓您參照學習。更希望您做完克漏字題目之後，能配合「寫作要點」或「短文解析」，再讀一次短文，以達到由閱讀中學習寫作的雙倍效果。

Cloze & Writing Practice

Table of Contents

Basic

Advanced

Cloze & Writing Practice

Being Healthy

Between the ages of nine and eighteen, you experience a series of physical changes called puberty. It sometimes causes problems. These __1__ skin problems, troublesome hair condition and also swings in mood. Sometimes you may feel very happy and confident and __2__ times you may feel unsure of yourself and your appearance.

__3__ the changes, you need to stay healthy. If your body is __4__ good condition, you will feel energetic, confident and able to deal with the __5__ of everyday life. Physical health can influence __6__ you feel about your looks. Your health shows in your __7__: a happy, healthy person has good skin and hair, and sparkle in the eyes.

Good health __8__ you better equipped to fight illness and resist infections. It also helps protect you __9__ certain diseases in adulthood, such as heart disease. These long-term benefits may seem unimportant when you are a young person, but there are also immediate benefits to __10__.

_____ 1. (A) include (B) exclude (C) show (D) result

_____ 2. (A) another (B) other (C) any (D) these

_____ 3. (A) To cope with (B) Coping with (C) Cope with (D) You cope with

_____ 4. (A) on (B) to (C) in (D) into

_____ 5. (A) do's and don'ts (B) ups and downs (C) ins and outs (D) right and wrong

_____ 6. (A) that (B) how (C) whether (D) why

_____ 7. (A) personality (B) character (C) appearance (D) mood

_____ 8. (A) has (B) offers (C) causes (D) makes

_____ 9. (A) not to get (B) to fight (C) from (D) away

_____ 10. (A) live healthy (B) keep healthy (C) living healthily (D) keeping healthily

 **原來如此**

1. **A** these 指上一句的 changes，這些問題包括 (include) 了…。
   (B) 排除在外 (C) 顯示 (D) 結果

2. **B** sometimes (有時候) 與 other times (其他時候) 為一組的搭配。

3. **A** To cope with... (為了要應付…) 以不定詞表達 you need to stay healthy 的目的。表目的不可用 V-ing。

4. **C** in good condition 情況良好

5. **B** ups and downs of life 生活的得意與失意 (起起落落)。
   (A) 該做與不該做的 (C) 詳細情形 (D) 是與非

6. **B** how you feel about your looks (你如何看待自己的外表) 為名詞子句，作為 influence 的受詞。

7. **C** 線索為 good skin and hair, and sparkle in the eyes；這些都是 appearance 的一部分。(A) 個性，人格 (B) 人格，角色 (D) 心情

8. **D** make (使得) + O + O.C.；better equipped (*adj.*) 作為受詞補語 (參考句式分析 2)。(C) cause + O + to V.。

9. **C** 要表達「保護…免於…」，用 protect + O + from 而非 protect + O + not + to V.。

10. **C** immediate benefits to... 對…立即的好處；to 是介系詞，之後要加名詞或動名詞作受詞。living healthily 活得健康；keep (保持) + Adj. (見句式分析 1)。

 **句式分析**

1 S + V. (feel, keep, stay, seem) + S.C.

You may feel very happy.
　　　　 V.　 S.C.

You need to stay healthy.
　　　　　 V.　 S.C.

These long-term benefits may seem unimportant.
　　　　　　　　　　　　　 V.　　 S.C.

(1) 以上三句中的 feel、stay、seem 為不完全不及物動詞，其後的 happy、healthy、unimportant 皆為形容詞，作為主詞補語 (S.C.)。

(2) 主詞補語可以是名詞或形容詞。

Extra 此類動詞有以下幾種：

(1) 「變得」：become、get、grow、turn、go

【例】He became a billionaire.

【例】She got very angry.

【例】The teacher grew impatient.

【例】My father's hair has turned completely gray.

(2) 「感官動詞」：look (看起來)、smell (聞起來)、taste (嚐起來)、sound (聽起來)、feel (覺得；摸起來)

【例】She looks younger than she is.

【例】The flowers smell good.

【例】The medicine tastes bitter.

【例】The story sounds interesting.

【例】I feel more confident now.

(3) 「似乎」：appear、seem

【例】The stranger appeared hungry and tired.

【例】The plan seemed impractical.

(4) 「保持，維持」：keep、stay、remain

【例】Keep silent.

【例】She exercises every day to stay fit.

【例】She remained single/unmarried.

---

2 S + make + O + O.C. (Adj./N/V/V-en)

Good health makes you better equipped to fight illness and resist infections.
　　　　　　　 V　　O　　　O.C.

(1) make 為不完全及物動詞，其句型為：

主詞 + 不完全及物動詞 + 受詞 + 受詞補語 (S + V + O + O.C.)

(2) make 的受詞補語除了是過去分詞之外，也可以是原形動詞、形容詞、或名詞。

a. 使得，使成為

【例】The atmosphere **made** me feel comfortable.

【例】The accident **made** the situation worse.

【例】We should do something to **make** Taiwan a better place to live.

【例】Drinking too much will **make** you drunk.

b. 命令

【例】The teacher **made** them listen carefully.

【例】The police **made** the man stop his car.

【例】My sister **made** me stay away from her stuff.

 問答

1. What's the main idea of this passage?

2. What problems do you have at the age of puberty?

3. What will help you deal with ups and downs of everyday life?

4. What do you do to make puberty less difficult?

 造句

1. to protect...from
   In winter, warm clothes <u>protect</u> us <u>from</u> the cold.

   _____

2. such as
   I like Italian food, <u>such as</u> pizza and pasta.

   _____

翻譯

1. 漫長的旅程使得他筋疲力盡。
   The long journey _____ .

2. 他變得更強壯更健康了。(grow)

   _____

3. 這料子摸起來很柔軟。
   The material _____ .

4. 這水果味道很可怕。(taste)

   _____

5. 意外發生時,務必要保持鎮定。

   _____

6. 這句子聽起來正確嗎?

   _____

Superstitions

Every culture in the world believes certain superstitions. Even societies that are very rational and ___1___ are sometimes a little bit superstitious. ___2___, the United States is a country that is very advanced in science and technology. But even in American society, people sometimes believe superstitions. They ___3___ "thirteen" an unlucky number. So, ___4___ rare to find a building of thirteen stories or a house with the number 13. You can imagine how they feel when Friday ___5___ on the thirteenth day of a month. The day is thought by a lot of people to be an unlucky day.

In addition to being superstitious about numbers, Americans often consider ___6___ unlucky to break a mirror. If a person breaks a mirror, he or she will have seven years of ___7___. Moreover, they always ___8___ walking under a ladder for fear of bringing themselves bad luck. Black cats are also unlucky especially when they cross people's path. A long time ago, people believed that black cats were really witches ___9___.

Some superstitions have become their customs. When someone sneezes, they say "God bless you." People ___10___ think that the soul would escape from the body when they sneezed. Being blessed can protect people from losing their souls.

_____ 1. (A) traditional   (B) scientific   (C) democratic   (D) independent

_____ 2. (A) For example   (B) However   (C) Moreover   (D) In addition

_____ 3. (A) regard   (B) think of   (C) consider   (D) describe

_____ 4. (A) they are   (B) they   (C) it is   (D) there is

_____ 5. (A) appears   (B) goes   (C) becomes   (D) falls

_____ 6. (A) that   (B) this   (C) they   (D) it

_____ 7. (A) performance   (B) misfortune   (C) resistance   (D) survival

_____ 8. (A) avoid   (B) permit   (C) allow   (D) suggest

_____ 9. (A) in disguise   (B) as proof   (C) under pressure   (D) on purpose

_____ 10. (A) may   (B) will   (C) used to   (D) are used to

原來如此

1. **B** 由下一句 advanced in science and technology 得知此題選 scientific。
2. **A** 由下文得知,舉美國為例。
   (B) 然而 (C) 再者,而且 (D) 此外
3. **C** consider + O + O.C. 參考句式分析 3;regard/think of + O + as + O.C.。
4. **C** it 為虛主詞,真主詞為 to find a building of... (參考句式分析 1)。
5. **D** fall on 表「節日或日子適逢某日」。
6. **D** it 為虛受詞,真受詞為 to break a mirror (參考句式分析 2)。
7. **B** 由前一句的 unlucky 得知此題選 misfortune (不幸)。
   (A) 表演 (C) 抵抗 (D) 倖存
8. **A** avoid (避免) + V-ing。
9. **A** 黑貓是女巫喬裝的 (in disguise)。
10. **C** 由後面的 would escape 得知需用表過去的字詞。used to V 以前常常…;be used to V-ing/N.P. 習慣於。

句式分析

1 **It + be + Adj./N (+ for sb) + to V...... (it 作虛主詞)**

It is rare to find a building of thirteen stories.

It is not a good idea to go there alone late at night.

(1) 以上兩句在主詞位置的 it 為虛主詞 (grammatical subject)。
(2) 真主詞是不定詞時,通常可把 it 放在句首,真正的主詞放在比較後面的位置。
(3) It is 之後可以接形容詞或名詞。
   【例】**It** is difficult for me to deal with such a person like him.
   【例】**It** is useless to persuade him to give it up.
   【例】**It** is a mystery how the world came into existence.

2 **S + consider/think/believe/find + O + O.C. (Adj./N)**

Americans consider "thirteen" an unlucky number.
              V   O   O.C.

consider、think、believe、find 常以形容詞或名詞作為其受詞補語。

【例】We consider him (to be) suitable for the job.

【例】Mr. Johnson thinks Jenny (to be) able to make it.

【例】We believe him (to be) innocent.

【例】The teacher found Adam (to be) a real genius.

UNIT 2

Extra regard/think of (認為) + O + as + O.C.

此類句型的動詞還有 view、see、recognize、describe、treat 等。

【例】We regard the mission as impossible.

【例】I think of him as a good leader.

【例】Traditionally people view women as mothers and housewives.

【例】The government recognized the MRT as the way to solve traffic problems in big cities of the country.

---

3 **S + V$_1$ + it + Adj./N + to V$_2$.... (it 作虛受詞)**

People consider **it** unlucky to break a mirror.

We consider **it** a great honor to be invited to give a speech here.

(1) 以上兩句在受詞位置的 it 為虛受詞 (grammatical object)。

(2) 當動詞之後有受詞及受詞補語，受詞是不定詞片語、that 子句或 wh- 子句時，通常把 it 放在受詞的位置，真正的受詞放在受詞補語之後。

(3) 此類句型的動詞常是 believe、consider、find、make、think 等。

【例】I believe it unkind to speak ill of him behind his back.

【例】We find it difficult to communicate with her.

【例】I made it a rule to take a walk before breakfast.

【例】Airplanes make it possible to travel around the world in a few days.

 問 答

1. What's the main idea of this passage?

2. Why do Americans think that black cats will bring them bad luck?

3. Write down just one sentence that tells about the superstition you believe.

造 句

1. to find
   I find him stingy and critical.

   _____

2. It is necessary...
   It is necessary for us to keep everything in order.

   _____

3. to find it impossible
   I find it impossible to master a foreign language in one or two years.

   _____

合併句子或改寫句子

1. { I pay him one million dollars.
   { He will not fix the CD player for me.
   Even if _____ .

2. { The engine made a lot of noise.
   { I was unable to fall asleep with it.
   The noise of the engine made it _____ .

3. { He will take my advice.
   { That is certain.
   It _____ .

4. Telling the difference between them is difficult for him.
   It _____ .

RoboShop

RoboShop, in downtown Tokyo, is the first store in the world where there are no
__1__ at work. Robots work 24 hours a day, __2__ the customers who come in.

RoboShop is like a __3__ vending machine. Customers come into the shop and
look at the __4__ cases. They write the numbers of the items they want on order
cards. Next, they punch the numbers into a machine __5__ to an ATM machine. Then
a robot, called Robo, goes to work.

Robo looks like a bucket __6__ wheels. It moves quickly around the store,
choosing items and putting them into a shopping basket. Robo always chooses the
biggest things first. If you buy a new toaster, Robo will not put it __7__ your fresh
sushi.

RoboShop sells many things that people buy every day, __8__ food and drinks
to household goods, magazines, and cosmetics. It __9__ sells many other things, such
as expensive watches and perfumes. RoboShop is just like a vending machine but
much bigger. Many people think it's interesting to shop there and the prices are lower
because the store doesn't have to pay __10__ to Robos.

_____ 1. (A) machines   (B) humans   (C) robots   (D) agents

_____ 2. (A) prepare   (B) preparing   (C) serve   (D) serving

_____ 3. (A) flat   (B) tiny   (C) giant   (D) expandable

_____ 4. (A) display   (B) performance   (C) description   (D) deposit

_____ 5. (A) familiar   (B) similar   (C) reliable   (D) valuable

_____ 6. (A) to   (B) by   (C) on   (D) in

_____ 7. (A) under   (B) below   (C) in the middle of   (D) on top of

_____ 8. (A) ranging   (B) offering   (C) from   (D) for

_____ 9. (A) also   (B) however   (C) thus   (D) yet

_____ 10. (A) debts   (B) salaries   (C) prices   (D) fines

 **原來如此**

1. **B** 由後文敘述得知在此工作的是 robots 而非 humans。
   (A) 機器 (C) 機器人 (D) 代理人

2. **D** 常用分詞構句句型 (參考句式分析 1)。

3. **C** 讀至最後一段第二句 much bigger 時即可確定此答案：giant 巨大的。
   (A) 扁平的 (B) 很小的 (D) 可擴充的

4. **A** 由下文得知顧客先看展示 (display)，再寫下物品編號，所以此處用 display cases。(B) 表演 (C) 描述 (D) 存款

5. **B** similar to an ATM machine 是形容詞片語，用以修飾 machine；be similar to 與⋯類似。(A) 熟悉的 (C) 可靠的 (D) 貴重的

6. **C** a bucket on wheels 裝上輪子的桶子；on 表示在⋯上面。

7. **D** on top of (在⋯之上)；由上句 Robo 會先選大件物品得知它不會把 toaster 放在 sushi 之上。

8. **C** from...to (從⋯到⋯) 表示 many things 的範圍。(A) 應改為 ranging from

9. **A** 除了上句的 goods (商品) 之外還有 many other things，因此選 also。

10. **B** the prices are lower 因為不用付店員薪水 (salary)。
    (A) 債 (C) 價格 (D) 罰款

句式分析

S + V₁..., V₂-ing/V₂-en....

Robots work 24 hours a day, serving the customers who come in.

分詞構句

It moves quickly around the stores, choosing items and putting them into a shopping basket.

分詞構句

兩個動作發生在同一時間，後面的動詞與分詞片語 (現在分詞或過去分詞) 表達附帶狀況。

【例】The students ran out of the classroom, laughing and shouting.

【例】She went out, slamming the door behind her.

【例】The dog stood at the door, barking at anyone passing by.

【例】She just sat there, doing nothing.

【例】The teacher sat there, surrounded by his students.

【例】She entered, accompanied by her mother.

UNIT 3

Extra 關於「分詞片語」：

(1) 可以放在名詞之後作為名詞的修飾語。功能與關係子句類似，但只限於與主動詞差不多同時發生的動作。

　　【例】Do you know the man sitting on the park bench? (...who/that is sitting...)

　　【例】Anyone breaking the rule will be fined two thousand dollars.
　　　　　(...who breaks...)

(2) 句中兩個動詞發生的時間有先後，通常不用分詞。

　　【例】Is there anyone who has finished your assignment?

　　【例】I need to talk to the student who broke the window yesterday.

(3) 過去分詞也有相同的用法：

　　【例】The old house built of wood and stone belonged to my grandfather.
　　　　　(...which was built...)

　　【例】The man taken away by the police robbed the convenience store last night.
　　　　　(...who was taken away...)

 問答

1. What's the main idea of this passage?

2. What do you often buy from vending machines?

3. What can you find in RoboShop?

4. Do you like the idea of buying things from RoboShop? Why or why not?

 造句

1. be similar to
   My cat is similar to yours in appearance.

　　_____

2. in fact
   Don't keep asking me if you did anything wrong. In fact, I am not sure about it.

　　_____

3. It is interesting....
   It is interesting to listen to pop music.

　　_____

Cloze Writing &
Practice

合併句子或改寫句子

1. {
They lay on the grass.
They were looking at the twinkling stars. (用 V-ing 合併)
}
They _____ .

2. {
She was playing the guitar.
She pretended not to see me. (用 V-ing 合併)
}
She _____ .

3. {
Who is the man?
The man is dancing with your sister. (用 V-ing 合併)
}
Who _____ .

4. {
Most of the students studied in the same school.
Most of the students were invited to the party. (用 V-en 合併)
}
Most of the students _____ .

翻譯

1. 他揮手道別。(wave his hand)

_____

2. 他挨家挨戶賣自製的冰淇淋。(home-made)
He walked _____ .

3. 小女孩安安靜靜地坐在地板上玩洋娃娃。(play with dolls)

_____

4. 隔壁住的是律師。
The man _____ .

5. 林太太出門了，留下女兒一個人在家。
Mrs. Lin _____ .

The Master of Mysteries

Alfred Hitchcock may be the most famous movie director ever. His movies are so popular because they ___1___ strong feelings in people who see the movies. Viewers often scream, laugh, shudder, or even close their eyes during different scenes.

Hitchcock was an expert ___2___ making viewers and characters feel anxious. His characters often get ___3___ in perilous situations that they don't understand. During these scenes, Hitchcock lets viewers know ___4___ the danger is. The audience want to warn the characters ___5___, but the characters can't take any notice of the warnings.

In most ___6___ movies, dangerous things happen in dark, scary places. But in Hitchcock movies, bad things usually happen in ___7___, "safe" places. For example, in the movie *The Birds*, a woman calmly sits in a park near a school. She doesn't know that birds are trying ___8___ her town. She sees one black bird sit on a jungle gym. The next time she looks, thousands of birds have gathered around her. Soon, the birds attack her and the school children.

Another part of Hitchcock's style is to put something ___9___ into a scary scene. He knew that people often laugh when they are scared. The funny parts in the movies add to the ___10___ that the audience feel while watching.

_____ 1. (A) find out   (B) bring out   (C) carry with   (D) die with

_____ 2. (A) in   (B) of   (C) with   (D) for

_____ 3. (A) exhausted   (B) known   (C) relieved   (D) caught

_____ 4. (A) that   (B) how   (C) what   (D) why

_____ 5. (A) to care about   (B) to watch out   (C) watching out   (D) taking care

_____ 6. (A) suspense   (B) blue   (C) action   (D) war

_____ 7. (A) dim   (B) light   (C) brighten   (D) gloomy

_____ 8. (A) leaving   (B) taking over   (C) to leave   (D) to take over

_____ 9. (A) humorous   (B) horrible   (C) thrilling   (D) serious

_____ 10. (A) joy   (B) humor   (C) tension   (D) curiosity

原來如此

1. **B** bring out 引發出來。(A) 發現 (C) 傳達
2. **A** 在 expert 之後用接 in 表「某方面的專家」。
3. **D** get caught in 遇到 (困境之類)。(A) 疲憊的 (C) 放心的
4. **C** 以 what the danger is 名詞子句 作為 know 的受詞；危險是「什麼 (what)」而不是「如何 (how)」。在 what the danger is 子句中，what 作為「主詞補語」。
5. **B** warn (警告) + O + to V (A) 在乎 (B) 當心 (D) 小心
6. **A** suspense movie (懸疑電影)，blue movie (色情電影)，horror movie (恐怖電影)；影片分類通常是 drama (劇情片)，comedy (喜劇片)，mystery (推理片)，action (動作片)。
7. **B** 由句首的 but 可得知此題要選與上一句的 dark 有相反之意的 light。
    (A) 微暗的 (C) 使明亮 (D) 昏暗的
8. **D** try + to V 設法或努力去⋯；try + V-ing 做看看會有什麼結果。
    由下文得知此題選 take over (佔據) 而非 leave。
9. **A** 由下一句 the funny parts in the movies 得知 Hitchcock 的風格是在恐怖之處加上有趣的部分，因此選 humorous。(B) 恐怖的 (C) 驚悚的 (D) 嚴肅的
10. **C** funny parts 目的在增加觀眾的緊張 (tension)。(A) 喜悅 (B) 幽默 (D) 好奇

句式分析

副詞子句簡化的分詞構句

The audience feel tension <u>while watching Hitchcock's movies</u>.
分詞構句

(1) while watching Hitchcock's movies 是一個保留「從屬連接詞」的分詞構句。
(2) 分詞構句是由副詞子句轉化而來的結構。
    a. 分詞構句中，分詞涵義上的主詞必須是主要子句的主詞。
    b. 最常代替表「時間」或「原因」的副詞子句。其位置可以在句首、句中、或句尾。
    【例】<u>Hearing the bad news</u>, he burst out crying.
        (= When he heard the bad news,...)
    【例】<u>Being a newcomer</u>, he was not familiar with everything here.
        (<u>As</u>/<u>Because</u> he was a newcomer...)

【例】 Walking on the beach, I found a purple shell. (= While I was walking...)

(3) 分詞構句可以保留從屬連接詞，使語意更明確。

【例】 **After** talking with my teacher, I felt more confident.

【例】 **While** watching TV, the old man fell asleep.

(4) 被動型態的分詞構句 (由副詞子句動詞的被動式可以辨別出用過去分詞)

【例】 **Written** in plain English, the book is suitable for beginners.

(= Because the book was written...)

【例】 **Disappointed** at the result, he shouted at his workmates.

(= Because he was disappointed...)

(5) 完成式型態的分詞構句 (having + V-en)

【例】 Having finished the assignment, he went to bed.

(= After he had finished...)

【例】 Having been bitten by a fierce dog, he refused to keep a dog as a pet.

(= Because he had been bitten...)

(6) 分詞的否定型態

【例】 **Not** knowing what to do, he turned to his teacher for help.

【例】 **Not** being able to finish it in time, he gave up in the end.

Extra

(1) 獨立分詞構句：兩個主詞不一致時使用，在分詞之前保留主詞。

【例】 It being a rainy day, they decided to stay home.

(= As it was a rainy day,...)

【例】 School being over, the students started to go home.

(= When school was over,...)

【例】 Weather permitting, we will go mountain climbing.

(= If the weather permits,...)

(2) 常用的類似獨立分詞結構用語，不受主詞一致的規則限制。

【例】 Generally speaking, men are stronger than women. (一般說來)

【例】 Taking everything into consideration, the project is acceptable. (一切都考慮之後)

【例】 Judging from his accent, he must be an Italian. (由…判斷)

【例】 Speaking/Talking of hobbies, I like playing basketball. (談到…)

另外有：broadly speaking (廣義地說)、frankly speaking (坦白地說)

 問 答

1. What's the reason that Alfred Hitchcock has always been popular?

2. What kind of movie is your least favorite? Why?

3. Talk something about the most recent movie that you saw.
   What was the title? Who starred it? What was it about?

1. for the first time
   <u>For the first time</u>, I went to visit the National Palace Museum.

_____

2. instead of
   <u>Instead of</u> staying in the classroom, he went out to play basketball.

_____

 合併句子或改寫句子

1. { He didn't know how to react.
    He kept silent. (用 V-ing 合併)

_____

2. Because he feared that he would be arrested, he tried to escape. (用分詞構句改寫)

_____

3. After he had failed twice, he decided not to try again. (用分詞構句改寫)

_____

翻譯

1. 因為病重，他取消英國行。(...cancelled his journey to...)

_____

2. 由於厭煩了我抱怨這節目，他關上電視。(get tired of; my complaint about)

_____

3. 由於不希望讓她生氣，我說了善意的謊言。(wish to make her...; a white lie)

_____

4. 因為覺得地板在搖動，我衝出我的房間。(shake; rush out)

_____

Homelessness

According to the United Nations, there are over 100 million homeless people worldwide. Where are they living? In places __1__ abandoned buildings, shelters, bus and train stations, subways, and city streets. Large cities such as New York and London can barely cope with large numbers of people __2__ on the streets.

It is impossible to estimate the exact number of homeless people because the conditions __3__ . Sometimes people are temporarily without a home __4__ a fire or a hurricane, for example. Sometimes people are forced out of their homes because they can't __5__ the rent. Others might have been living on the streets for years. It is not easy to count them. Nor __6__ easy to describe a typical homeless person, for the picture has changed over the years and differs from place to place.

What are the __7__ of homelessness? For some, it is simply a __8__ of affordable housing. Many of the homeless have lost their jobs and are poor. Many others have problems __9__ drugs or alcohol. Some have left home because the __10__ there were bad. Others are mentally ill, discharged from hospitals with nowhere to go. They have no family and no one they can __11__ .

There are some suggestions made to solve the problem, but it does take time to __12__ an end to this problem in sight.

_____ 1. (A) unlike   (B) like   (C) to like   (D) alike
_____ 2. (A) live   (B) to live   (C) living   (D) for living
_____ 3. (A) vary   (B) lessen   (C) increase   (D) worsen
_____ 4. (A) result from   (B) result in   (C) because   (D) because of
_____ 5. (A) take   (B) pay   (C) extend   (D) attach
_____ 6. (A) is it   (B) it is   (C) are they   (D) they are
_____ 7. (A) facts   (B) causes   (C) figures   (D) results
_____ 8. (A) need   (B) tendency   (C) lack   (D) trend
_____ 9. (A) with   (B) for   (C) to   (D) of
_____ 10. (A) situation   (B) environment   (C) services   (D) conditions
_____ 11. (A) help   (B) control   (C) turn to   (D) change to
_____ 12. (A) come   (B) put   (C) take   (D) go

 **原來如此**

1. **B** like 為介系詞，此處用法和 such as 類似。(A) 不像 (C) 喜歡 (D) 相同的

2. **C** living on the streets 是由關係子句 (who live on the streets) 轉化而來的分詞片語，修飾 people。

3. **A** 以下三句敘述造成 homeless 不同的原因，因此此題選 vary (不同，差異)。(B) 減少 (C) 增加 (D) 惡化

4. **D** 此處為 because of + N 作為 O 的用法；另外 because 也可以直接加子句。(A) 由…造成的 (B) 造成…

5. **B** pay the rent 付租金。(A) 接受 (C) 延伸 (D) 繫上或附上

6. **A** nor 為否定用語，放在句首造成主詞和動詞倒裝 (參考句式分析)。

7. **B** 本段其他的句子都在談 homelessness 的原因，因此選 cause。(A) 事實 (C) 數字 (D) 結果

8. **C** 無家可歸的原因是缺乏他們負擔得起的住宅，因此此題選 lack (缺乏)。

9. **A** have a problem with... 有…的困難

10. **D** 離家原因是家中情況不好，因此選 conditions (情況)。又因動詞是 were，因此不選 A 或 B。

11. **C** no one (whom) they can turn to；turn to sb. 向…求助。

12. **B** come to an end (結束) 的用法是 something comes to an end。而 put an end to 的用法是 put an end to something，故本題為 (B)。

句式分析

倒裝句

Nor is it easy to describe a typical homeless person.

此句是倒裝句。nor 是否定詞置於句首，造成動詞 is 在前、主詞 it 在後，主動詞倒序的結構。

倒裝句句型有兩種：
1. 和疑問句相同 (助動詞在主詞之前) 的句型：
   (a) 「否定用語」not、no、neither、nor、seldom、little、hardly、scarcely、never、rarely、nowhere、by no means、in no way、under no circumstances 等在句首的倒裝：
   【例】**Not** a sound <u>did he make</u>.

【例】I didn't see it, **nor** did anybody else.

【例】**Never** in my life have I seen such a wonderful sight.

【例】**Rarely** have I been more careful.

【例】**No** sooner had he arrived home than the telephone rang.

【例】**Not** only did he show us how to do it but he offered to help us.

【例】**Not** until I left home did I realize that home was the sweetest.

(b)「Only + 副詞用語(片語或子句)」在句首的倒裝：

【例】**Only** by working hard can you succeed.

【例】**Only** when he is in trouble will he realize how important friendship is.

(c) so、such、to such a degree 等表「強調」的詞語在句首的倒裝：

【例】**So** great was his surprise that he couldn't utter a word.

【例】**Such** was his joy that he skipped around the classroom.

2. 整個「動詞置於主詞之前」的句型：

(a) 地方副詞置於句首，動詞是不及物動詞時的倒裝：

【例】**Under** the bed was lying my black cat.

【例】**On** the bench sat an old woman with her white dog.

(b) 方向介副詞 in、out、on、off、up、down、away、along 之後，動詞是不及物動詞，主詞不是代名詞時的倒裝：

【例】**Away** went the car.

【例】**Down** went the sun.

 問答

1. What's the main idea of this article?

2. Where are the homeless living in your city?

3. What cause them to be homeless?

 造句

1. Nor...
She can't speak Japanese. Nor can I.

___

2. Only then...
Only then did I realize how forgetful he was.

___

3. Some...Others

Some stayed to reconstruct their hometown. Others left and never returned.

_____

4. It takes time/patience/effort...

It takes patience to take care of babies.

_____

合併句子或改寫句子

1. { He finished his dinner.
   { Someone knocked on the door.
   Hardly _____.

2. { He is an excellent surgeon.
   { He also plays the piano very well.
   Not only _____.

3. He seldom tells us about his past experience.
   Seldom _____.

4. He was so confused that he didn't know what to do.
   So _____.

翻譯

1. 他只有日夜工作才可以賺到足夠的錢。
   Only by _____.

2. 我從未聽過這麼美的聲音。
   Never _____.

3. 我絕不會洩漏秘密。
   By no means _____.

4. 他正對面坐著一個年輕女孩。
   Directly opposite him _____.

Multimedia Matchmaking

Computers are very helpful in our everyday lives. Can you imagine they work as a matchmaker? Recently, they have helped make the __1__ for a suitable life partner a lot easier. All over the world, computer-assisted dating has become a very good business. Time gets shorter and requirements get higher: most people cannot afford the time it __2__ to get to know someone, nor the __3__ of a blind date. So, for a modest fee, your personal data, __4__ your likes and dislikes, are entered into a computer program that will produce a list of names of people that might __5__ you. All you need to do is __6__ the necessary phone calls.

If you are willing to spend more money, a video of you is made, __7__ you talk about yourself, and the kind of person you would like to meet. The video is then imported into a computer and candidates can __8__ their partners on a screen. If you have your own PC, you can have __9__ to the system through the Internet. For an extra fee you'll be able to see the __10__ of potential candidates in the comfort of your home. And, if all goes well, you may __11__ inviting your computer to be your best man or bridesmaid at your wedding __12__ .

1. (A) decision	(B) search	(C) expectation	(D) image
2. (A) gives	(B) offers	(C) takes	(D) brings
3. (A) benefit	(B) possibility	(C) risk	(D) cause
4. (A) instead of	(B) together with	(C) included	(D) added
5. (A) match	(B) represent	(C) neglect	(D) misunderstand
6. (A) make	(B) take	(C) to get	(D) to reach
7. (A) that	(B) in that	(C) which	(D) in which
8. (A) choose	(B) take	(C) copy	(D) meet
9. (A) way	(B) tendency	(C) measures	(D) access
10. (A) opinions	(B) background	(C) images	(D) material
11. (A) object to	(B) end up	(C) apply for	(D) look into
12. (A) anniversary	(B) publication	(C) ceremony	(D) celebration

原來如此

1.	**B**	由上一句 matchmaker 得知「電腦的工作在幫助人找合適的伴侶」，因此此題選 search。search for (尋找)。(A) 決定 (C) 預期 (D) 形象
2.	**C**	做某事需要時間所用到的句型是 it takes time to do something；此題 the time 之後關係代名詞 that 省略，that it takes to get to know someone 為關係子句修飾 the time (參考句式分析 1)。
3.	**C**	nor (也不) 此處指也擔不起盲目約會 (blind date) 的風險 (risk)。 (A) 利益，好處 (B) 可能性 (D) 原因
4.	**B**	你的個人資料連同喜好，因此此題選 together with (介系詞用法)。由此題前後的逗點，以及之後的動詞 are 得知此題不是動詞的位置，故不選 (C) 或 (D)。(A) instead of 代替，而不
5.	**A**	match you (與你相配)。(B) 代表 (C) 忽視，疏忽 (D) 誤會
6.	**A**	All you need to do is + (to) V；打電話是 make a phone call。
7.	**D**	in which you talk... 是「非限定用法」的關係子句 (見句式分析 2)
8.	**A**	從螢幕上選擇伴侶，因此此題選 choose。
9.	**D**	have access to (可接近，可利用…)。(B) 傾向 (C) 措施，處置
10.	**C**	由本段第一句 a video of you is made 得知可以看到應徵者的影像面貌 (image)。(A) 意見 (B) 背景 (D) 資料
11.	**B**	end up (by) doing something 最後做了…。(A) 反對 (C) 申請 (D) 調查
12.	**C**	由此句的 all goes well, you may end up inviting your computer to be your best man or bridesmaid 得知此題應選 wedding ceremony (結婚典禮)。 (A) 週年 (B) 出版 (D) 慶祝

句式分析

1 限定用法的關係子句

Your personal data are entered into a computer program that will produce a list of
　　　　　　　　　主要子句　　　　　　　　　　　　　　關係子句
names of people that might match you.
　　　　　關係子句

兩個關係子句各自修飾之前的名詞 program 及 people。

(1) 關係代名詞具有連接兩個句子的功能

　【例】That's the person. He lives next door to us.

➜ That's the person who lives next door to us.

(當以上兩句合併之後，可以看出關係代名詞 who 的兩種功能。它有代名詞的功能代替了 he，又有連接的功能，將兩個句子連接起來。)

(2) 常用的關係代名詞有指人的 who、whose、whom、that，有指事或物的 which、that。

【例】The man who/that is standing at the desk is our math teacher.

【例】The lady whose handbag was robbed was my aunt.

【例】The magazine which/that I borrowed from you is very informative.

(3) 關係子句所修飾的名詞前面有限定性質的形容詞 the first、the last、the only、the same、the very、all、no 時，常用關係代名詞 **that**。

【例】She is the best actress that has ever acted here.

【例】The only thing that you have to do is to find a job.

【例】All that glitters is not gold.

(4) 在「限定用法」的關係子句中受格關係代名詞常可省略。

【例】The doctor (whom/that) you visited yesterday is very famous.

(5) 在「介系詞」之後的關係代名詞只能用 whom, which 且不能省略。

【例】I don't like the man with whom you have been working.

【例】I don't like the house in which you live.

2 非限定關係子句 (1)

A video of you is made, in which you talk about yourself.
非限定用法的關係子句

(1) 在形式上非限定用法的關係子句要用逗點和其他部分分開，限定用法則不必。
The boy that I danced with at Nancy's birthday party was coming to see us.
句中限定用法的關係子句 that I danced with at Nancy's birthday party 指出了哪一個男孩，就如同 the girl in blue jeans、the book on the windowsill 中，in blue jeans 和 on the windowsill 的「限定功能」。

(2) I met Mr. White, **who** invited us to his birthday party.
句中「非限定用法」的關係子句 who invited us to his birthday party 只是做額外的補充說明，Mr. White 已經很明白指定了某一個人。
此用法的主要功能在「連接句子」。因此上一句可以改寫為 I met Mr. White, **and** he invited us to his birthday party.

(3) 非限定用法的關係代名詞不能用 that，即使是受格也不省略。

問 答

1. What's the main idea of this passage?

2. What is a blind date?

3. What do matchmakers do?

4. Why has computer-assisted dating become a very good business?

造句

1. All you need to do...
   All you need to do is wait and see.

2. prefer to...rather than
   I prefer to sit here until day breaks rather than (to) take sleeping pills.

合併句子或改寫句子

1. { The statue is a work of art.
   { The statue stands in the center of the park.
   The statue _____ .

2. { The author wrote the book.
   { The author is a neighbor of ours.
   The author _____ .

3. { My father-in-law has been in a nursery home for 5 years.
   { He suffers from Parkinson's disease.
   My father-in-law _____ .

翻譯

1. 他願意在我不在時照顧我的貓。(be willing to + V)

2. 你能想像他年輕時多帥嗎？
   Can you imagine _____

3. 這個母親冒生命危險從火場救出嬰兒。(at the risk of the life)

New Eating Habits

Statistics compiled by the USDA (United States Department of Agriculture) show that red meat, which used to be the most popular choice for dinner, is no longer an American favorite.   1 , chicken, turkey, and fish have become more popular.   2   of these foods have greatly increased in recent years. This is probably a result of the   3   of the danger of eating food that contains high levels of cholesterol or animal fat. Doctors believe that cholesterol is a   4   to human health.

Americans also change their eating patterns to   5   the needs of different situations. They have certain ideas about which foods will increase their athletic ability, help them lose   6 , make them alert in a meeting, or put them   7   the mood for romance. For example, Americans choose pasta, fruit, and vegetables, which   8   them with carbohydrates, to give them   9   to do physical activities. Adults choose foods   10   fiber, such as bread and cereals, for breakfast, and salads for lunch to prepare them for business appointments. For romantic dinners, however, Americans choose shrimp and lobster. While many of these ideas   11   nutritional facts, some are not.

Americans' awareness of nutrition, along with their changing tastes and needs, leads them to consume a wide   12   of foods for health, for fun, and simply for good taste.

_____	1. (A) For instance	(B) Besides	(C) Instead	(D) As a result
_____	2. (A) Nutrients	(B) Sales	(C) Production	(D) Consumption
_____	3. (A) preparation	(B) application	(C) proposal	(D) awareness
_____	4. (A) supposition	(B) threat	(C) protection	(D) cure
_____	5. (A) provide	(B) meet	(C) attend	(D) keep
_____	6. (A) faith	(B) patience	(C) weight	(D) temper
_____	7. (A) in	(B) on	(C) with	(D) for
_____	8. (A) give	(B) offer	(C) tend	(D) supply
_____	9. (A) effort	(B) image	(C) strength	(D) defect
_____	10. (A) contain	(B) include	(C) rich in	(D) short of
_____	11. (A) are caused by	(B) are based on	(C) put emphasis on	(D) result from
_____	12. (A) sort	(B) number	(C) variety	(D) various

 原來如此

1. **C** 由上下文 red meat...is no longer an American favorite..., chicken, turkey, and fish have become more popular 得知此題選 instead (反而)。
   (A) 例如 (B) 除此之外 (D) 結果

2. **B** 由上一句 chicken...become more popular 得知此類食物銷售 (sales) 增加。由此句動詞 have increased 得知主詞要是複數形，sales 是主詞。
   (A) 營養物 (C) 生產 (D) 消費

3. **D** the awareness of the danger 對危險的認知。(A) 準備 (B) 應用 (C) 提議

4. **B** cholesterol 對 human health 是一項威脅，因此選 threat (威脅)。
   (A) 假定 (C) 保護 (D) 治癒

5. **B** 符合需要是 meet the needs。(A) 供給 (C) 出席 (D) 保持

6. **C** lose weight 減重，其他選項與文意不合。(A) 信心 (B) 耐心 (D) 脾氣

7. **A** 有…的心情是 in the mood for something/to do something。

8. **D** supply someone with something 供應某人某物。

9. **C** physical activities (體能活動) 需要力氣，因此選 strength。
   (A) 努力 (B) 形象 (D) 缺點

10. **C** rich in fiber (含有豐富纖維) 是形容詞片語修飾 foods。此為修飾語的位置，不能選原形動詞。(A) contain (包含) 與 (B) include (包括) 均為動詞 (D) 缺少…

11. **B** 由此句後半部的 some are not，得知此句的結構是 while many are..., some are not。be based on (以…作根據；根據…) 指觀念是根據事實而來。
    (A) are caused by (由…造成的) 與文意不合 (C) 注重 (D) 由…造成

12. **C** a (wide) variety of 及 various (*adj.*) 都指各種各類的。用法是 a variety of foods/various foods。

句式分析

1 「非限定」關係子句 (2)

His son fooled around doing nothing, **which** made him angry.
➔ His son fooled around doing nothing, **and that** made him angry.

He killed his own child, **which** shocked everyone that knows him.

(1) 關係代名詞在「非限定用法」中可以指前面整個句子。

(2) 關係代名詞前面有「數量詞」(one、two、three、half) 或是「定詞」(some、any、all、several、many、none) 或是「最高級」時也是非限定用法。

【例】He has three daughters, <u>two of whom</u> / <u>and two of them</u> are school teachers.

【例】There are five old houses in this town, <u>one of which/and one of them</u> was built of wood.

【例】Every year, tens of thousands of tourists come to this summer resort, <u>the majority of whom/and the majority of those people</u> are Japanese.

2 wh- 子句

They have certain ideas about **which** foods will help them lose weight.

(1) which 子句是「間接問句」，作為 about 的受詞。

【例】I worried about **what** might happen to her.

(2) 但是 idea 之後的 about 可以省略。

【例】Do you have any idea (about) **where** she lives?

【例】I have no idea (about) **what** I can do to please you.

 問答

1. What's the main idea of this article?

2. Why does red meat become the less popular choice for dinner?

3. Why do we need food that can supply us with carbohydrates?

4. What foods are rich in fiber?

 造句

1. a variety of

Our library has a wide variety of books.

2. be based on

The movie is based on an Irish legend.

 合併句子或改寫句子

1. {
The young man kidnapped his uncle.
That made all his relatives furious. (用 which 合併)
}
The young man _____ .

2. {
I saw several women in the park.
All of them were doing some exercise. (用 whom 合併)
}
I _____ .

3. {
The famous writer is invited to the party.
That made everyone excited. (用 which 合併)
}
The famous writer _____ .

翻譯

1. 她通過了測驗，此事使她父母以她為榮。(which; be proud of her)

_____

2. 我一點都不知道她把金子藏在哪裡。
I don't have the slightest idea _____ .

3. 凡是來參加會議的人都可以得到禮物。(attend the meeting; will be given a present)

_____

4. 這個展覽室裡的任何東西都是無價的。(the showroom; priceless)

_____

Animal Communication

Although body language is an important part of animal mating rituals, it is a vital means of communication in many other situations, too. Many animals have greeting rituals. When different members of the same species meet in the wild, they may be uncertain __1__ they are facing an enemy or a friend. So they go through careful greeting rituals to make sure that the other animals do not intend to __2__ .

Other animals make special signals to __3__ the members of their species if there is danger nearby. One kind of deer in North America has a white tail. When it is frightened, it runs away with its white tail __4__ upright in the air. The other deers see this warning sign and know that they should run away, too.

Honey bees use body signals to __5__ information. They spend the summer collecting pollen and nectar from flowers __6__ honey. If a bee finds a large group of flowers, it returns to the hive. There it "dances," flying around in a __7__ eight, wriggling and shaking its body as it __8__ so. When the others see these movements, they learn where the flowers are and fly out to __9__ the pollen.

Like humans, animals also express their moods and feelings through __10__ expressions. Chimpanzees open their mouths __11__ and show their teeth when they are frightened or excited. They often stick out their lips as a sign of greeting and press their lips __12__ when they want to look threatening.

_____ 1. (A) that   (B) which   (C) of which   (D) whether
_____ 2. (A) attend   (B) attack   (C) survive   (D) arrest
_____ 3. (A) warn   (B) greet   (C) make   (D) find
_____ 4. (A) hold   (B) holding   (C) to hold   (D) held
_____ 5. (A) acquire   (B) gather   (C) pass on   (D) pass away
_____ 6. (A) making   (B) gathering   (C) to make   (D) to gather
_____ 7. (A) clue   (B) line   (C) figure   (D) circle
_____ 8. (A) is   (B) does   (C) can   (D) will
_____ 9. (A) require   (B) produce   (C) make   (D) harvest
_____ 10. (A) wise   (B) startled   (C) facial   (D) embarrassed
_____ 11. (A) wide   (B) widely   (C) big   (D) greatly
_____ 12. (A) together   (B) apart   (C) away   (D) on

 原來如此

1.	**D**	whether/whether...or 用法參考句式分析 2。
2.	**B**	動物透過問候方式來確定對方無攻擊企圖，因此選 attack (攻擊)。
		(A) 出席 (C) 活下來 (D) 逮捕
3.	**A**	make special signals 的目的是警告 (warn) 同類。(B) 打招呼
4.	**D**	with 用法見參考句式分析 1。
5.	**C**	pass on information 傳遞訊息。(A) 獲得 (B) 收集 (D) 死去
6.	**C**	此處用不定詞片語 to make honey 表達 collecting pollen and nectar 的目的。make (製造)，gather (收集)。
7.	**C**	a figure eight「8 這個數字」。(A) 線索 (B) 直線 (D) 圓圈
8.	**B**	as it does so 代替 as a bee dances，用助動詞 does 用來代替前面提過的動詞 dances，而不是用 is、can、will。
9.	**D**	bees fly out to harvest (收成) the pollen；此句中 harvest 與 collect 同義。
		(A) 需要 (B) 製造
10.	**C**	由下兩句 open their mouths wide and show their teeth 等得知此題應選 facial expression (臉部表情)。(A) 智慧的 (B) 驚嚇的 (D) 尷尬的
11.	**A**	把嘴巴或眼睛張大用 open the mouth/eyes wide，用 wide 而不用 big。
		(B) 廣泛地
12.	**A**	press something together 把…擠壓在一起。(B) 分開地

 句式分析

1 with/without + O + O.C. (V-ing/V-en/Adj./Particle)

It runs away with its white tail **held** upright in the air.

Tony looked at the pretty girl with his face **turning** red.

(1) 用 with 片語表達伴隨主動詞 run away 及 look at 發生的狀況。
(2) with 片語通常是 with + N + V-ing/V-en/Adj./Particle (介副詞)。
(3) 使用現在分詞或過去分詞須視受詞與受詞補語為主動關係或被動關係而定。如第一個例句中，受詞 its white tail 與受詞補語 held 為被動關係。例句二中的受詞 his face is turning red，故用現在分詞 turning。

【例】 Don't talk **with** your mouth full of food. (形容詞片語)
【例】 He slept **with** the light on. (介副詞)

30

2 whether/whether...or...

They may be **uncertain** <u>whether</u> they are facing an enemy or a friend.

I **doubt** <u>whether</u> she will offer help.

(1) whether 引導名詞子句時，whether 子句除了可作為<u>主詞</u>之外，也常作<u>受詞</u>放在：
  a.「形容詞」之後，例如 uncertain、not sure。
  b.「動詞」之後，例如 ask、know、doubt、wonder。
  c.「介系詞」之後，例如 about、on、of、to。
  【例】I am **not sure** <u>whether</u> the situation is getting worse.
  【例】The boy **asked** his teacher <u>whether</u> he liked baseball or not.
  【例】It depends **on** <u>whether</u> you insist or not.
  【例】Mom is worried **about** <u>whether</u> you are safe or not.

(2) **whether + to + V** 為名詞子句簡化為名詞片語的用法。當前後主詞相同時，可省略主詞及助動詞。此用法常放在一些動詞之後，例如 know、ask、tell、wonder、understand 等。
  【例】I am **wondering** <u>whether</u> to stay home or go to a movie with you.

(3) 以下為不可以用 if 代替 whether 的情況：
  a. 在介系詞之後
  b. whether + to V
  c. whether 子句在句首
  d. whether or not

(4) whether 之後有 or/or not 時，如下列第一句比較常用 whether，尤其在正式文體中。第二及第三句則不可用 if。
  【例】I doubt <u>whether</u> he will come to see us <u>or not</u>.
  【例】I doubt <u>whether or not</u> he will come to see us.
  【例】I am uncertain <u>whether</u> to stay <u>or</u> leave.

問答

1. What's the main idea of this passage?

2. In what situation does the deer with a white tail hold its tail upright in the air?

3. How does a bee tell the other bees the place the flowers are found?

4. What may be chimpanzees' facial expression when they want to attack their enemies?

造句

1. to make sure

   I want to <u>make sure</u> that she will be responsible for it.

   _____

2. to doubt if/whether

   I doubt *if*/*whether* this is what he needs.

   _____

3. <u>With/Without</u> + O + O.C.

   Stella left the kitchen <u>with the kettle boiling</u>.

   _____

改寫句子

1. We are uncertain of his presence. (用 whether 子句改寫)

   _____

2. { He lay there.
   { His eyes were fixed on the ceiling. (用 with 片語改寫)
   He _____ .

翻譯

1. 她一句話也不說，很生氣地走開了。(..., without a word...)

   _____

2. 人類常用臉部表情表達情緒。(...tend to...facial expressions)

   _____

3. 火車轟隆隆地經過，我聽不見你說話。(...with the train...; roar along)

   _____

4. 我不確定他是否要吃中藥。

   I'm not sure _____ .

Anger of the Sun

A hundred years ago, sun-tanned skin was not fashionable. Tanned skin usually meant that a person worked in the sun. Farmers, construction workers and cowhands all had tans. More educated people worked in the office, so their skin did not get ___1___. In fact, many people tried to protect their skin from the sun ___2___ people would think that they were educated. Men wore hats with large brims, and women carried beautifully embroidered parasols to ___3___ the rays of the sun.

Later in the twentieth century, tanned skin became much more fashionable. Young people everywhere sat in the sun for hours, turning from side to side ___4___ a perfect tan. A tan was then all the fashion: only wealthy people could spend a lot of free time in the sun!

However, the sun's rays can cause changes ___5___ the cells of the skin. There are many cases of cancer in Arizona and other sunny places like Queensland, Australia. Skin cancer is a very serious disease in which abnormal cells grow ___6___. So people today shield their skin from the sun. Doctors ___7___ several ways to protect the skin.

① ___8___ the sun between 10 a.m. and 3 p.m. This is the time when the sun's rays are strongest and most dangerous.

② Use sunscreen—a ___9___ lotion with an SPF (sun protection factor) of at least 15.

③ Wear ___10___ clothing. Wide-brimmed hats, long-sleeved shirts, and long pants or skirts will protect skin from the sun.

_____	1. (A) lighter	(B) brighter	(C) darker	(D) fresher
_____	2. (A) so that	(B) for fear that	(C) since	(D) once
_____	3. (A) keep away	(B) fall into	(C) make up	(D) face with
_____	4. (A) getting	(B) get	(C) got	(D) to get
_____	5. (A) for	(B) in	(C) to	(D) at
_____	6. (A) under control	(B) out of control	(C) up to date	(D) out of date
_____	7. (A) forbid	(B) conclude	(C) apply	(D) recommend
_____	8. (A) Amplify	(B) Alter	(C) Avoid	(D) Ascend
_____	9. (A) detective	(B) protective	(C) receptive	(D) attentive
_____	10. (A) appropriate	(B) intensive	(C) loose	(D) tight

原來如此

1. **C** 接受高教育的人從事辦公室工作，所以皮膚比較不容易曬黑，因此此題選 darker (膚色較深的)。(A) 較輕的 (B) 較明亮的 (D) 較新鮮的

2. **A** others would think that they were educated 為 protect the skin from the sun 的目的，因此選表目的的從屬連接詞 so that。
   (B) 以免 (C) 自從，既然 (D) 一旦

3. **A** 撐洋傘的目的是「阻擋光線」，因此選 keep away (阻擋，使遠離)，此處不定詞片語表目的。(B) 開始 (C) 捏造 (D) 面對

4. **D** 用不定詞 to get 表達 turning from side to side 的目的。

5. **B** change in something 指在某方面的改變。

6. **B** 由前面的 abnormal cells 得知細胞失去控制 (out of control)。
   (A) 在…掌控中 (C) 流行 (D) 落伍

7. **D** 醫生推薦防曬的方法，因此此題選 recommend (推薦)。
   (A) 禁止 (B) 下結論 (C) 申請

8. **C** avoid the sun 指避開陽光。(A) 擴大 (B) 改變 (D) 向上昇

9. **B** sunscreen 是保護性的 lotion，因此選 protective。
   (A) 警探 (C) 易接受的 (D) 注意的

10. **A** 由下文 wide-brimmed hats, long-sleeved shirts, ... 得知要穿適當的衣物，因此選 appropriate (適當的)。(B) 密集的 (C) 鬆的 (D) 緊的

句式分析

1 關係副詞的用法：...N + why/when/where + S + V...

This is the **time when** the sun's rays are strongest and most dangerous.
關係子句

(1) 在指時間的名詞 time、day、year …之後，用關係詞 **when** (代替了 at/in/on/during which) 引導關係子句。
   【例】Sunday is the day when I am least busy.

(2) 在指地方的名詞 place、city、house、office …之後，用關係詞 **where** (代替了 at/in/on/from which) 引導關係子句。
   【例】This is the place where the accident happened.

(3) 在指理由的名詞 reason 之後，用關係詞 **why** (代替了 for which) 引導關係子句。
   【例】Nobody knows the reason why Mr. Wang got angry.

(4) 但是在表方法的名詞 the way 之後用 **in which**。

　　【例】 I am not sure of <u>the way in which</u> he coped with the problem.

(5) 而 that 常常用來代替以上所用到的關係詞 (when、where、why、in which)，that 也可以省略。

　　【例】 Sunday is <u>the day</u> (that) I am least busy.

　　【例】 This is <u>the place</u> (that) the accident happened.

　　【例】 Nobody knows <u>the reason</u> (that) he got angry.

　　【例】 I am not sure of <u>the way</u> (that) he coped with the problem.

2 as + adj. (+ N)/adv. + as + { one can/could / possible }

　　【例】 Please try to make your speech **as** <u>brief</u> **as** <u>you can/possible</u>.

　　【例】 Come home **as** <u>soon</u> **as** <u>you can/possible</u>.

　　【例】 To broaden knowledge, you should read **as** <u>many books</u> **as** <u>you can/possible</u>.

　　【例】 He worked day and night to earn **as** <u>much money</u> **as** <u>he could/possible</u>.

Extra **it is/was...that...** 分裂句

把要強調的句子部分 (可以是主詞、受詞、地方副詞、時間副詞) 放在 It <u>is/was</u> 和 <u>that</u> 之間，其餘放在 that 之後。

【例】 <u>Nelson</u> ran across <u>our English teacher</u> <u>at MRT station</u> yesterday.

➡ It was <u>Nelson</u> that ran across our English teacher at MRT station yesterday.

➡ It was <u>our English teacher</u> that Nelson ran across at MRT station yesterday.

➡ It was <u>at MRT station</u> that Nelson ran across our English teacher yesterday.

➡ It was <u>yesterday</u> that Nelson ran across our English teacher at MRT station.

 問 答

1. What's the main idea of this article?

2. Why did tanned skin become fashionable later in the 20th century?

3. Why do people today tend to protect their skin from the sun?

4. When is the time the sun's rays are strongest and most dangerous?

5. What clothing will you choose to wear if you have to stay in the scorching sun?

 造句

1. .... so that...

   I stayed up late <u>so that</u> I could read more.

   _____

2. out of control

   The fire was <u>out of control</u> and killed many people.

   _____

3. as...as possible

   Please come here <u>as early as possible</u>.

   _____

 合併句子或改寫句子

1. { This is the place.
   { They store something valuable. (用 where 合併)

   _____

2. { I like the way.
   { Jane organized the class reunion in this way. (用 that 合併)
   I _____ .

3. Tell me the reason for your absence. (用 why 改寫)

   _____

翻譯

1. 大雨使我們無法去健行。(keep...from; take a hike)

   _____

2. 盡量多閱讀。(as...as one can)

   _____

3. 她盡可能走快一點以便趕上我們。(as...as possible; catch up with)

   _____

The Loss of the Titanic

The great ship, the *Titanic*, sailed for New York from Southampton on April 10th, 1912. She was carrying 1,316 passengers and a ___1___ of 891. At that time, she not only was the largest ship that had ever been built, ___2___ was regarded as unsinkable, for she had sixteen watertight compartments. ___3___ two of these were flooded, she would still be able to float. However, the tragic sinking of this ship would always be remembered, for she went down ___4___ her first voyage with heavy ___5___ of life.

On April 14th, ___6___ the *Titanic* was sailing across the icy waters of the North Atlantic, a huge iceberg was suddenly ___7___ by a lookout. After the alarm had been given, the great ship turned sharply ___8___ a direct collision. However, she still collided with the iceberg. Suddenly, there was a trembling sound from ___9___ , and the captain went down to see what had happened. The noise had been ___10___ that no one thought that the ship had been damaged. The captain realized, ___11___ his horror, that the *Titanic* was sinking rapidly, for five of her sixteen watertight compartments had already been flooded! The order to ___12___ ship was given and hundreds of people plunged into the icy water. As there were not enough lifeboats for everybody, about 1,500 lives were lost.

_____ 1. (A) crowd   (B) crew   (C) herd   (D) flock
_____ 2. (A) and   (B) so   (C) then   (D) but
_____ 3. (A) Because   (B) Even if   (C) Even   (D) Whether
_____ 4. (A) on   (B) with   (C) in   (D) to
_____ 5. (A) amount   (B) load   (C) loss   (D) burden
_____ 6. (A) and   (B) but   (C) while   (D) if
_____ 7. (A) presented   (B) spotted   (C) reminded   (D) overlooked
_____ 8. (A) to reject   (B) rejecting   (C) to avoid   (D) avoiding
_____ 9. (A) above   (B) below   (C) inside   (D) outside
_____ 10. (A) very slight   (B) very harsh   (C) so faint   (D) so deafening
_____ 11. (A) to   (B) with   (C) for   (D) in
_____ 12. (A) abandon   (B) protect   (C) maintain   (D) fix

 原來如此

1.	**B**	crew (全體船員) 是集合名詞。
		(A) 群眾 (C) (牛，馬) 群 (D) (羊，鳥) 群；人群
2.	**D**	not only...but (also) 參考句式分析2。
3.	**B**	由本句文意得知此處需要表即使的從屬連接詞 even if，even (甚至於) 是副詞。(A) 因為 (D) 是否
4.	**A**	on her first voyage 在她第一次航行中
5.	**C**	heavy loss of life 傷亡慘重 (損失)。(A) 量 (B) 裝載，負荷 (D) 負擔
6.	**C**	由之後的 was sailing 及此句文意得知此題選表時間的從屬連接詞 while。
7.	**B**	iceberg 被發現，因此選 spot (認出)。(A) 呈現 (C) 提醒 (D) 俯視；忽略。
8.	**C**	to avoid (為了避免) 在此表目的。reject (拒絕)。
9.	**B**	由其後的 the captain went down to see 得知此題選 below (在下方)。
10.	**C**	so...that (非常…結果…) 由此句文意得知聲音微弱 (faint)。
		(A) 微弱的，輕微的 (B) 刺耳的 (D) 震耳欲聾的
11.	**A**	to his horror 令他恐懼的是 (參考句式分析1)
12.	**A**	由之後的文意得知下達了棄船的命令。(A) 拋棄 (C) 維持，維修 (D) 修理

句式分析

1 to one's + N (形容情緒的名詞)

The captain realized, **to his horror**, that the *Titanic* was sinking rapidly.

to his horror 作「令他恐懼的是」解，句子其他部分則把恐懼的事表達出來。

> 類似的片語有：
>
> to one's disappointment (令…失望的是)
> to one's joy/delight/pleasure (令…喜悅的是)
> to one's sorrow/grief/distress (令…傷心的是)
> to one's surprise/shock/astonishment (令…驚訝的是)
> to one's satisfaction (令…滿意的是)

這些名詞都是表達情緒方面的，通常放在句首作「令某人感到…的是」。此外，可用 great 或 much 來加強語氣。

【例】To my disappointment, he gave in to their demands.

【例】To our relief, the mountain climbers returned to their school.

【例】Much to our surprise, he survived after drifting in the sea for ten hours.

2 not only...but (also)

She **not only** was the largest ship **but (also)** was regarded as unsinkable.
　　　不僅　　　　　　　　　　　　　　　　　　而且

與 not only...but also... 類似的對等連接詞用法有：either...or... (不是…就是…)；neither...nor... (既不…也不…)；both...and... (既…又…)。成對出現的「對等連接詞」(coordinators) 使用時要特別注意前後對稱，也就是前後連接相同性質的句構。

【例】She not only *sings* beautifully but also *plays* the guitar very well.

【例】Either *you leave my car* or *I'll call the police.*

【例】Neither *you* nor *I* have the right to destroy it.

3 so...that
so that

The noise had been **so faint that** no one thought that the ship had been damaged.
　　　　　　　　　　　非常…結果…(表結果)

They tried to protect their skin **so that** people would think that they were educated.
　　　　　　　　　　　　　　　為了…(表目的)

(1) so...that/such...that + 副詞子句 (表結果)，意為「如此…以致於…」。so 後面接形容詞或副詞，such 接名詞。

　　【例】It rained so heavily (that) we had to cancel the game.

　　【例】He is so nice (that) whoever knows him likes him.

　　　➔ He is such a nice person/so nice a person (that) whoever knows him likes him.

(2) so that/in order that + 從屬子句 (表目的)，後面接表「目的」的子句，表示「為了…以便…」，子句中常使用助動詞 will、would、can、could 等來修飾語氣。

　　【例】I'm going to leave earlier so that I will not get caught in the traffic jam.

　　【例】She turned off the stereo so that everyone there could hear clearly.

問答

1. What is the story about?

2. Why was the Titanic considered to be unsinkable?

3. Why were 1,500 people finally drowned?

1. to one's disappointment
   To Henry's disappointment, his girlfriend refused to marry him.

2. while
   I read your book while you were taking a shower.

3. so that
   Take an umbrella so that you won't get wet.

改寫句子

1. She was too poor to afford a meal. (用 so... that 改寫)

2. I exercise a lot to keep in shape. (用 so that 改寫)

3. He finished the complicated work on his own and this surprised me.
   To my   .

4. In addition to the piano, she also plays the cello. (用 not only...but also... 改寫)

翻譯

1. 令我們欣喜的是所有乘客都生還了。(survived)
   To our   .

2. 她太虛弱無法再走遠了。(so...that)

3. 他聽音樂的時候睡著了。(...while...)

Body Painting

In many cultures, people decorate their bodies with pictures and designs. Sometimes, the human body is printed or colored with dye, which can be washed off later. Other forms of body decoration, such as tattoos, are __1__ and stayed with the wearer for life. Very often, people decorate their bodies for a particular purpose, which is __2__ in the types of pattern that they use.

The Indians of North America __3__ general use of body painting. When warriors prepared for battle, they would paint themselves with __4__ design. They concentrated on their faces which were decorated with red stripes, black masks or white circles around the eyes. These designs made the warrior look __5__ and aggressive. Other people also used war-paint. When the Romans __6__ Britain, they found that the Ancient Britons painted themselves with blue called woad before going into battle.

Body painting can be used for occasions __7__ battles. The Aboriginal peoples of Australia often decorate their bodies with bold white markings for a corroboree. A corroboree is a special meeting __8__ men dance and sing.

The Maoris of New Zealand decorated their bodies with tattooing. This long-lasting form of body decoration indicated the social status of an individual. __9__ important a person was, the more tattoos he had. Some chiefs and kings had their faces __10__ entirely by tattoos.

_____ 1. (A) lengthy   (B) heavy   (C) temporary   (D) permanent
_____ 2. (A) pictured   (B) imagine   (C) reflected   (D) refreshed
_____ 3. (A) did   (B) had   (C) made   (D) took
_____ 4. (A) bold   (B) timid   (C) rough   (D) mild
_____ 5. (A) reliable   (B) funny   (C) fierce   (D) gentle
_____ 6. (A) left   (B) invaded   (C) escaped   (D) sneaked
_____ 7. (A) in spite of   (B) instead of   (C) other than   (D) more than
_____ 8. (A) at which   (B) of which   (C) in that   (D) for that
_____ 9. (A) How   (B) However   (C) The less   (D) The more
_____ 10. (A) to be covered   (B) covered   (C) cover   (D) to cover

 原來如此

1.　**D**　由之後的 stayed with the wearer for life 得知此題選 permanent (永久的)。
　　　(A) 冗長的 (B) 重的 (C) 暫時的
2.　**C**　目的被「反映」出來，reflect (反映，反射)。
　　　(A) 想像，描繪 (B) 想像 (D) 使精神舒暢
3.　**C**　make use of 利用，使用
4.　**A**　戰士要去打戰，需要「顯眼的」(bold) 圖案。bold 也有「大膽」的意思。
　　　(B) 膽小的 (C) 粗糙的 (D) 溫和的
5.　**C**　圖案使戰士看起來很勇猛，因此選 fierce (兇猛的)。
　　　(A) 可靠的 (B) 有趣的 (D) 溫和的
6.　**B**　羅馬人侵略 (invade) 英國。(C) 逃走 (D) 偷偷溜進
7.　**C**　身體彩繪可以用在戰爭以外的情況，因此選 other than (除…之外)。
　　　(A) 儘管 (B) 代替
8.　**A**　在會議中是 at the meeting，因此選 at which (參考 Unit 6 句式分析 1)。
9.　**D**　the + 比較級 , the + 比較級 (參考句式分析 1)
10.　**B**　have + O + O.C. 參考句式分析 2。

 句式分析

1 **the +** 比較級 **, the +** 比較級

The more important a person was, the more tattoos he had.

此句等於 When a person was more important, he had more tattoos.
【例】The harder you work, the more likely you are to succeed.
　　➔ If you work harder, you are more likely to succeed.
【例】The more we get together, the happier we'll be.
　　➔ If we get together more, we'll be happier.
【例】The sooner we begin our work, the earlier we will finish it.
　　➔ If we begin our work sooner, we will finish it earlier.

UNIT 11

2 S + have + O + V (原形)/V-ing/V-en

Some chiefs and kings **had** their faces **covered** entirely by tattoos.

have + O + V (原形)/V-ing/V-en 此種用法中 have 的語意是：
叫某人或使得某人做某事或表經歷某事。
此句由 their faces 和 cover 的關係判斷用 covered (V-en)，亦即從 their faces were covered by tattoos 的被動關係判斷。
【例】 **Have** him get a copy of that magazine.
【例】 The entertainer **had** us all laughing.
【例】 He **had** his hair cut very short.
【例】 He **had** his computer stolen.
【例】 I won't **have** you getting/get around here. (won't have 表不准)

Extra | **whether S + V, ...**
S₁ +V₁ + whether + S₂ + V₂

(1) Whether she will be with us or not, I have decided to go.
　　　　不論她是否陪我們…
(2) I don't know whether she will be with us.
　　　　　…她是否會陪我們

例句 (1) 是副詞子句表「讓步」的用法，指 whether 子句中的事不會對主要子句的事造成影響。
例句 (2) 是名詞子句作 know 的受詞 (參考 Unit 8 句式分析 2)
此類用法還有：whatever (no matter what)、whoever (no matter who)、whichever (no matter which)、wherever (no matter where)、whenever (no matter when)。
【例】 Whatever (=No matter what) you do, I'll support you.
【例】 Whoever (=No matter who) comes, tell him I am away.
【例】 Wherever (=No matter where) you go, you'll find 7-Eleven.
【例】 Come here whenever (=No matter when) you like.

 問答

1. What is the main idea of this article?

2. What do the Aboriginal peoples in Australia do at a corroboree?

3. Why did the Maoris of New Zealand have tattoos?

4. Now in Taiwan there are still some people who have their bodies tattooed. What might be the reason?

造句

1. whatever

   <u>Whatever</u> you say, I won't believe you.

2. (ever) since

   We've been friends <u>ever since</u> we met at senior high school.

3. to get rid of

   Do something <u>to get rid of</u> the paparazzi.

改寫句子

1. If you get together more, you'll have more in common. (the + 比較級, the + 比較級)

2. As you climb higher, you will see farther. (the + 比較級, the + 比較級)

3. In spite of the fact that the job is very difficult, I am determined to do it on my own.

   However _____.

翻譯

1. 你讀得越多，就獲得越多知識。(knowledge)

2. 她怎麼吃都不胖。

   However _____.

3. 他把「愛」這個字刺在手臂上。

   He had the word _____.

4. 不管你同不同意，他堅持要出國。(insist on)

   Whether _____.

Cartoons

Every morning millions of people struggle out of bed, fumble into some clothing, __1__ their way to the morning newspaper. Many of them turn their half-opened eyes __2__ the comics section of the newspaper.

Cartoons reflect the times and the troubles and worries of the people. They give people an opportunity to __3__ themselves and at familiar situations. They also __4__ the problems that people make for themselves—like making a problem out of which type of car to buy. In hard times—times of economic troubles—people want someone to __5__ their troubles on. Cartoons provide scapegoats. They also help people to see the humor in a not-so-funny situation. For example, a cartoon might say that the government of a country is __6__ the bad economy and also show the government leaders as a group of ridiculous people. This makes people feel better about their situation.

Cartoons also make people laugh at their own personal worries. Young people who are not always sure of __7__ to act can smile at their awkwardness. Old people whose grown children pay little attention to them can chuckle at their __8__. Students who have studied too little before an examination can laugh at their __9__. Everyone's problems are made bigger-than-life in the comics. Perhaps the problems seem funny because __10__ humor in something that is real but is made unreal.

_____ 1. (A) making   (B) finding   (C) and make   (D) to find
_____ 2. (A) to   (B) from   (C) with   (D) in
_____ 3. (A) play jokes on   (B) laugh at   (C) punish   (D) forgive
_____ 4. (A) make fun of   (B) find fault with   (C) take advantage of   (D) get rid of
_____ 5. (A) owe   (B) cause   (C) blame   (D) scold
_____ 6. (A) satisfied with   (B) dissatisfied with   (C) disappointed at   (D) responsible for
_____ 7. (A) what   (B) how   (C) where   (D) whether
_____ 8. (A) curiosity   (B) pride   (C) loneliness   (D) content
_____ 9. (A) hesitation   (B) courage   (C) anxiety   (D) confidence
_____ 10. (A) there is   (B) it is   (C) if there is   (D) which is

 原來如此

1.　**C**　三個一連串的動作是用「A, B, and C」的方式表達。因此用 and make 而非 making。make one's way to 前往某處。

2.　**A**　turn one's eyes to 把目光轉向某處。

3.　**B**　由之後的 and at 可以確定此題需要有 at 的片語 laugh at。
　　　(A) 開玩笑 (C) 處罰 (D) 原諒

4.　**A**　由上下文得知 cartoons 有趣的一面是取笑自己，因此選 make fun of (取笑)。(B) 挑剔 (C) 利用 (D) 除掉

5.　**C**　blame...on someone 歸咎…於某人。(A) 欠 (B) 造成 (D) 責罵

6.　**D**　由前文 blame the troubles on 得知要某些人負責，因此選 responsible for (為…負責)。(A) 對…滿意 (B) 對…不滿意 (C) 對…失望

7.　**B**　how to act (如何表現)，act 作「表現」時是不及物動詞。how 是疑問副詞表「以…方法」；what 是疑問代名詞，例如 what to do，do 涵義上的受詞就是 what，因此不選 (A)。疑問詞 + 不定詞當名詞片語用，whether to act 語意不合。

8.　**C**　由之前的 pay little attention to them 得知老人的寂寞 (loneliness)。
　　　(A) 好奇 (B) 驕傲 (D) 滿意

9.　**C**　由學生考前 study little (準備不充分)，得知此題選 anxiety (焦慮)。
　　　(A) 猶豫 (B) 勇氣 (D) 信心

10.　**A**　funny 的原因是其中有幽默，因此選 there is。不需重複使用「從屬連接詞」，因此不選 (C)。

 句式分析

wh- 疑問詞 **+ to V**

They also make fun of the problems that people make for themselves——like making a problem out of **which** type of car to buy.
　　　　　　　　　　　　　　　　　　　　名詞片語

Young people who are not always sure of **how** to act can smile at their awkwardness.
　　　　　　　　　　　　　　　　　　　名詞片語

(1) 底線部分是由疑問詞 which 和 how 之後接不定詞組成的名詞片語，作為介系詞 of、about 的受詞。

　　【例】Here is the information about where to shop in this city.

【例】The scientists have made their final decision of <u>where to search for fossils</u>.

【例】She has no idea of <u>how to cope with stress</u>.

【例】They presented a discussion of <u>what files to download</u>.

(2) 在 wonder、find out、know、explain、ask、tell、consider、show、discover、understand、show 及其他類似語意的動詞之後，也可接<u>疑問詞＋不定詞</u>作為這些動詞的受詞。

【例】Could you tell me <u>where to find a vending machine</u>?

【例】I didn't know <u>when to meet Jane</u>.

【例】The child wondered <u>who to play with</u>.

【例】The student doesn't know <u>what to do in case of emergency</u>.

Extra

1. **not...until**

   He **didn't** realize the importance of exercise **until** he had a pain in his back.

   not...until 直到…才；此句還可以用下列兩種句型表達：

   【例】It was **not until** he had a pain in his back <u>that</u> he came to realize the importance of exercise.

   【例】**Not until** he had a pain in his back <u>did he come</u> to realize the importance of exercise.

2. **As soon as...., S + V....**

   As soon as I entered the music hall, the concert began.

   as soon as (一…就…) 是表時間的從屬連接詞，相同用法的連接詞還有：

   the moment、the minute、the second、the instant

   此句也可以用 no sooner...than; <u>hardly/scarcely</u>...<u>when/before</u> 表達。

   【例】I had no sooner entered the music hall than the concert began.

   【例】I had <u>hardly/scarcely</u> entered the music hall <u>when/before</u> the concert began.

3. **that 子句**

   Some people still believe **that** more education will create more equal opportunities.

   The belief **that** more education will create more equal opportunities has been proved wrong.

   (1) 比較兩句：兩個 that 子句都是名詞子句，第一句的 that 子句做 believe 的受詞。
       第二句的 that 子句是<u>用來補充說明</u> belief，稱作同位語。

   (2) 在 belief、fact、news、proof、suggestion、statement、theory、conclusion、idea 等名詞後面的 that 子句都是做同位語用的名詞子句。

       【例】I am not aware of the <u>fact</u> **that** he is the sponsor.

       【例】They have come to the <u>conclusion</u> **that** he neglected his duty.

       【例】They have a <u>dream</u> **that** one day Nantou will again be a safe and beautiful <u>place to live in</u>.

造句

1. as soon as

   <u>As soon as</u> he got out of bed, the earth began to tremble.

   _____

2. The minute

   <u>The minute</u> she saw me, she ran away swiftly.

   _____

 合併句子或改寫句子

1. { He lost his right hand.
    { He kept on learning to play basketball.
   Although _____ .

2. You will not finish it in time if you don't burn the midnight oil. (用 unless 改寫)

   _____

3. He did not face the music until he found he had no other choice.

   It was not until _____ .

翻譯

1. 老太太不知道如何使用手機。(wh- 疑問詞 + to)

   The old lady didn't know _____ .

2. Fiona 提議我下課後該去公園慢跑。(...suggestion that...)

   Fiona gave the suggestion _____ .

3. 我到達車站的時候，火車剛好離開了。

   I _____ the train left.

4. Willa 已經決定何時要去逛街了。

   Willa has made a decision of _____ .

5. 小男孩在雨停後才離開這家商店。(...not......until...)

   _____

NOTE

Knitting for Penguins

A common hobby in the Australian island state of Tasmania is knitting sweaters. But not just any sweaters! All over Tasmania, volunteers knit tiny sweaters for penguins!

Penguins are flightless birds that live in the Southern Hemisphere, including Tasmania, an island at the bottom of Australia. They __1__ on fish and they spend much of their time in the water, __2__ they nest and lay their eggs on land. Penguins cannot fly, but they have special feathers that keep them warm and waterproof in the freezing water. But when they are __3__ by an oil spill, the oil clogs their feathers and they can no longer keep warm. Also, in an __4__ to clean themselves, they lick the oil off their feathers. __5__ can poison the penguins so that they become very sick and die.

While wearing the sweaters, the penguins can stay warm and dry, and __6__ from eating the oil on their feathers. Last year, over fifteen thousand sweaters were knitted by volunteers in Tasmania and all over the world, to be kept in reserve __7__ a major oil spill.

If you are a keen knitter and would like to contribute, the pattern for a penguin sweater is available __8__ the Internet. The sweaters should be made from pure wool, and knitted by hand quite __9__ . Loose knitting can __10__ holes in the sweater where the penguin's beak or flipper might become caught. It doesn't matter __11__ color the sweaters are, but usually knitters choose attractive styles to suit the most fashionable of penguins. They look especially cute in stripes. Usually penguins look __12__ they are wearing a black and white dinner party suit (even the female penguins), but when wearing their sweaters they look much more __13__ !

_____ 1. (A) insist   (B) try   (C) attend   (D) feed

_____ 2. (A) because   (B) as   (C) although   (D) if

_____ 3. (A) defended   (B) affected   (C) painted   (D) dyed

_____ 4. (A) attempt   (B) attainment   (C) assurance   (D) insurance

_____ 5. (A) Which   (B) They   (C) This   (D) Those

_____ 6. (A) recover   (B) recovered   (C) protected   (D) protect

_____ 7. (A) because of   (B) in honor of   (C) instead of   (D) in case of

_____ 8. (A) in   (B) to   (C) on   (D) under

_____ 9. (A) beautifully   (B) firmly   (C) seriously   (D) closely

_____ 10. (A) adapt to   (B) deal with   (C) result in   (D) result from

_____ 11. (A) what   (B) whether   (C) either   (D) any

_____ 12. (A) alike   (B) as   (C) as if   (D) even if

_____ 13. (A) casual   (B) formal   (C) casually   (D) formally

NOTE

原來如此

1. **D** 由空格後 fish (企鵝的食物) 得知此格選 feed (以…為食)。

2. **C** 空格前後兩個子句的邏輯關係很清楚：雖然在陸地上 (on land) 築巢生蛋卻大部分時間在水中 (in the water) 中活動。

3. **B** 企鵝受漏油事件影響 (affected)，(A) 防衛 (D) 染色

4. **A** 企鵝 lick the oil off 是嘗試 / 企圖 (attempt) clean themselves。
   (B) 達成 (C) 保證 (D) 保險

5. **C** This 這個代名詞可以指上一句提到的事 (lick the oil off their feathers)。

6. **C** protect (*v.t.*) 用法是 protect + O + from/against，此格前面有 stay (連綴動詞)，stay protected 就如同被動式 (are protected) 一樣。

7. **D** to be kept in reserve 是線索，儲備以防 (in case of) 還有重大漏油事件。

8. **C** 在網路上就是用 on the Internet。

9. **B** 下一句的 loose (鬆鬆的) knitting 是線索，空格就選反義的 firmly。(D) 密切地 / 親密地。

10. **C** 空格之後的文意是 loose knitting 造成的後果，result in (造成…結果)，result from (由…造成的)。

11. **A** It 是虛主詞，含意上的主詞是 what color the sweaters are，其他選項都不可能成為名詞子句，參考句式分析 1。

12. **C** look as if S + V... 是一種比喻的用法；在非正式的用法中 look like S + V... 是可以的 (參考句式分析 3)。

13. **A** dinner party suit (晚宴裝) 是線索，這是正式場合的衣服。相對地穿 sweaters 時看起來就 casual 多了，因為 look (連綴動詞)，此格要選 adj. 而非 adv.。

句式分析

1 後面接 wh- 子句作為真正的主詞〔it 為虛主詞〕

It doesn't matter what color the sweaters are.

It doesn't matter whether you will succeed in something.

It doesn't matter (無關緊要，一點都沒關係) 後面接 wh- 子句作為真正的主詞〔it 為虛主詞 (grammatical subject)〕。

【例】**It** doesn't matter what your friends told you about me.

【例】Does **it** matter how long my hair is or what color my skin is?

【例】 **It** doesn't matter <u>how many copies of the album have been sold</u>.

❷ Although

They feed on fish and they spend much of their time in the water, <u>although</u> they nest and lay their eggs on land.

I like Joseph, <u>although</u> I've never seen him.

(1) although 是從屬連接詞，在以上兩句中相當於 <u>but/and yet</u> 的用法。
(2) 而以下兩句中的 although 則是可以用 <u>though</u> 來代替。

　　【例】 <u>Although/Though</u> I am poor, my life is as rich as a billionaire.
　　【例】 <u>Although/Though</u> beauty may be in the eye of the beholder, the feeling of being beautiful exists only in the mind of the beheld.

❸ as if／as though

Penguins look <u>as if/as though</u> they, even the female penguins, <u>are wearing</u> a black and white dinner party suit.

She looks <u>as if/as though</u> she <u>hasn't eaten</u> anything for three days.

(1) 以上兩句的在非正式用法中可以用 like 代替。注意子句中的動詞時態，這和假設語氣無關，因為句子暗示：第一句「企鵝的毛色讓牠們看起來的確像穿晚宴裝」，第二句「她看起來真的很餓」。
(2) 以下的 as if 子句的動詞就是假設語氣的用法：

　　【例】 He often talks **as if** he <u>were</u> our supervisor.
　　　　　(事實上他不是；這是與現在事實相反的假設)
　　【例】 He looked startled **as if** he <u>hadn't planned</u> on being seen.
　　　　　(事實是他刻意要被人看到；這是與過去事實相反的假設)

問 答

1. What's the main idea of this article?

2. Why would penguins' lives be threatened by an oil spill?

3. Why should the sweaters be firmly knitted by hand?

造句

1. no longer

   The student is <u>no longer</u> allowed to borrow books from the school library.

   _____

2. It doesn't matter

   <u>It doesn't matter</u> how you will redecorate your room.

   _____

3. in case of

   Be sure to know what to do <u>in case of</u> an earthquake.

   _____

4. Although

   <u>Although</u> she was highly qualified, she didn't get the admission to the program.

   _____

翻譯

1. 這個傷害你的人是否值得被原諒沒什麼關係。原諒是你給自己的禮物。

   _____ the person _____ deserves to be forgiven.

   Forgiveness is _____ .

2. 他的舉止好像他擁有這家餐廳。(own)

   He behaved _____ .

3. 1960 年發生在智利的地震造成超過 6000 人死亡。

   _____ in Chile in 1960 _____ .

4. 雖然她有時候脾氣壞，他還是喜歡她。

   He likes her _____ .

NOTE

The Origin of Surnames

Surnames were first used to distinguish people with the same names. English surnames have __1__ from various sources. Most surnames have evolved from four general sources: occupation, location, father's name, and characteristic.

Surnames __2__ from occupations for centuries. For example, the woodworker was called __3__, the bricklayer was called Mason and the man who made barrels was called Cooper. Besides, almost every village had a blacksmith, so Smith became one of the most popular surnames.

There are many other surnames __4__ from locations. If people lived over the hill, they would become known as Overhill. If they resided near a __5__, they might be identified as Brook. You can recognize a location name because it ends with a __6__ word, such as "-hill," "-wood," or "-brook." However, not all endings are so easily recognizable. Surnames that end in "-ton," "-ham," or "-stead" mean a farm, __7__ endings such as "-leigh" or "-ley" mean a clearing.

However, other surnames come from a father's name. __8__, a person named Jackson means that he is the son of Jack, and Peterson is the son of Peter. Lastly, many surnames were earned because of __9__ characteristics. If a person was short in height, he might simply be called Short. If he was tall, he could be called Longfellow. As for Kennedy, in Celtic languages it means "ugly head". When someone had the characteristic of an animal, he or she might have the name of Fox if he was __10__.

Now, when you hear a surname, you know more about the origin and you can even tell a person something more about his or her ancestors.

_____ 1. (A) traced   (B) originated   (C) inherited   (D) devoted

_____ 2. (A) caused   (B) was caused   (C) have been derived (D) have derived

_____ 3. (A) Butcher   (B) Underwood   (C) Taylor   (D) Carpenter

_____ 4. (A) originating   (B) originated   (C) rising   (D) arose

_____ 5. (A) gulf   (B) stream   (C) cliff   (D) waterfall

_____ 6. (A) historic   (B) biological   (C) geographic   (D) artistic

_____ 7. (A) when   (B) while   (C) because   (D) though

_____ 8. (A) In other words   (B) For example   (C) As a result   (D) On the contrary

_____ 9. (A) facial   (B) family   (C) psychic   (D) physical

_____ 10. (A) sly   (B) loyal   (C) timid   (D) weak

NOTE

1. **B** 空格後的 sources (來源) 是線索，此格選 originated (起源)。
   (A) 追溯 (C) 繼承 (D) 致力於
2. **C** 由下兩句文意可知這個主題句中的動詞要用是 be derived (源自)，因為 for centuries 表示至今有好幾世紀之久，所以要用現在完成式。
3. **D** 線索是 woodworker 所以選 carpenter (木匠)。(A) 屠夫 (C) 裁縫
4. **A** 選 originating 是因為句子結構 (參考句式分析 1)。(C) 升起 (D) 起源於
5. **B** 線索是 brook (溪流)，故選 (B) 溪流、小河。(A) 海灣 (C) 懸崖 (D) 瀑布
6. **C** 線索是 "hill," "-wood," or "-brook" 這些都是有關地理的 (geographic)。
   (A) 歷史的 (B) 生物的 (D) 藝術的。
7. **B** 空格前後列出不同的字尾做對照，因此選表示對照的從屬連接詞 while。(參考句式分析 2)
8. **B** 線索是前句的 father's name，空格之後的是所舉的例子，所以選 For example。
9. **D** 線索是之後的 short, tall, ugly head，這些都是身體的 (physical) 特徵。
10. **A** 英文裡就用 fox 形容人狡猾 (He is a sly old fox.)。

1 There is/are + N + V-ing/V-en....

There are many other surnames <u>originating</u> from locations.

There were a lot of kids <u>running and laughing</u> at the playground.

以上兩句真正的主詞是 surnames 和 kids，動詞是 are 和 were，是由「主動語態」動詞轉換為「現在分詞」；若為「被動語態」，動詞則轉換成「過去分詞」。

【例】 There are many people at the station <u>waiting</u> for the bus.

【例】 There is a girl in the shop <u>helping</u> her mother at the checkout.

【例】 There are 26 to 30 thousand people <u>murdered</u> in the US every year.
   (判斷用現在分詞或過去分詞的關鍵在於主詞和之後動詞的關係：
   people are waiting for the bus; a girl in the shop is helping her mother at the checkout; people are murdered)

2 while

Surnames that end in "-ton" or "-ham" mean a farm, while endings such as "-leigh" or "-ley" mean a clearing.

while 這個從屬連接詞在句中表達對照的關係，即比較兩種同類。

【例】I like rock 'n' roll, while my husband likes classical music.

【例】China is rich in mineral wealth, while Japan is scarce in it.

【例】Some students are good at English, while others are not.

3 because of

Many surnames were earned **because of** physical characteristics.

The student was asked to leave **because of** violating the school rules.

(1) **because of** 是介系詞用法，後面接名詞片語或動名詞片語做為受詞。

【例】They envy us **because of** our freedom.

【例】These patients are dying **because of** lack of access to life-saving drugs.

Extra **because** 是從屬連接詞，後面要接子句。

【例】You can recognize a locational name **because** it ends with a geographic word.

【例】They said so **because** they hate our way of life.

【例】More than 18,000 Americans die every year only **because** they cannot afford private health care insurance.

問答

1. How many sources of surnames are mentioned in this article? What are they?

2. Which of the following are locational names? _____
   Which of the following are occupational names? _____

(A) Miller	(B) Nickson	(C) Cook	(D) Newport	(E) Green
(F) Bradley	(G) Barton	(H) Armstrong	(I) Parker	(J) Norwood
(K) Thompson	(L) Bush	(M) Baker		

3. What might be the characteristic of the person who was given the name, Brown?

造句

1. because of

   They don't care how many Iraqis have died <u>because of</u> the war and occupation.

   _____

2. because

   I'll do all I can to support you <u>because</u> you are worth it.

   _____

3. There is/are... + V-ing

   <u>There are</u> a group of small children <u>playing</u> hide and seek in the garden.

   _____

4. be derived from

   It is important that any fresh meat should <u>be derived from</u> safe sources.

   _____

翻譯

1. 這個地區有三個居民因為吃了野禽死於禽流感 (because of)。

   Three _____ bird flu _____

   wild fowls.

2. 在墓園裡有他的三個朋友靜靜地對他致敬。

   There were three of his friends at the yard _____

   respects to him.

3. Jane 認為自己太瘦，計畫兩個月內增胖四磅，而 Joyce 卻想盡快減重。

   Jane thinks she is too thin and _____

   _____ .

4. 一般人都相信 SARS 源自中國。(originate)

   It is believed that SARS _____ .

Chatsworth House Farm and Park

The 1,000 acres of park and farmland surrounding Chatsworth House in Derbyshire, England, can be enjoyed throughout the year. However, they __1__ season by season. In spring, farmyard animals like pigs, cows, sheep, chickens and goats have their young. You can go for a springtime woodland walk to see these animals, the wild flowers and newly __2__ trees as well.

In summer, there are special animal displays and "Meet the Animals" sessions. These __3__ cow and goat-milking demonstrations, and people can stroke and hold the young lambs and chickens. __4__ the weather is warm, there are trailer rides through the Stand Wood forest area. __5__ the arrival of autumn, the leaves will turn brilliant gold and then fall from the trees. Woodland walks are one of the best ways to see these bright autumn colors.

Winter is colder than the other seasons and activities move __6__. A craft cottage is open daily so you can make country-style Christmas decorations and cards. You can join in activities such as Christmas stories, plays and songs inside, while outdoors there are still tractor rides around the farm if the weather is __7__.

The wide rambling park is open every day of the year. People can walk, picnic or play throughout the park and also along the Derwent River which __8__ through the park. __9__ the farmyard, the park is a wild place which people are free to walk through anytime during daylight hours. Traditional and modern sculptures __10__ through the park and gardens, and small lakes and curving walkways are in full view of everyone in the park. This is a lovely way to enjoy the great English countryside.

_____ 1. (A) fade	(B) grow	(C) change	(D) develop
_____ 2. (A) budded	(B) felled	(C) sprouting	(D) uprooting
_____ 3. (A) hold	(B) include	(C) conclude	(D) wrap
_____ 4. (A) Only	(B) Even	(C) As soon as	(D) As long as
_____ 5. (A) With	(B) Without	(C) Before	(D) After
_____ 6. (A) forward	(B) downward	(C) indoors	(D) outdoors
_____ 7. (A) freezing	(B) pleasant	(C) foggy	(D) bleak
_____ 8. (A) runs	(B) dams	(C) rises	(D) floods
_____ 9. (A) Besides	(B) Unlike	(C) Beyond	(D) Through
_____ 10. (A) are dotted	(B) are created	(C) erected	(D) covered

UNIT 15

NOTE

....

....

....

....

....

....

....

....

....

原來如此

1.　**C**　由第一、二、三段內容得知不同季節景象就會「改變」。(A) 褪色
2.　**C**　新發芽的是 newly sprouting 或 newly budding。(B) 砍倒 (D) 連根拔起
3.　**B**　these 指 displays 和 sessions，它們包括 (include) 擠牛乳和羊乳的現場表演。(A) 容納 (C) 總結 (D) 把…包裹起來
4.　**D**　由句子結構來判斷，此格要放「連接詞」，(A)(B) 都是副詞。(C) 一…就
5.　**A**　with 指「隨著」之意。
6.　**C**　線索是「冬天天氣變冷」及下一句的「工藝品小木屋提供室內的活動」。
7.　**B**　tractor rides 的活動需要有好天氣的條件。
　　　　(A) 非常冷的 (B) 舒適的 (C) 多霧的 (D) 陰冷的
8.　**A**　run through 流經某處。(B) 築水壩 (C) 升起 (D) 氾濫
9.　**B**　這句敘述的是 park 和 farmyard 不同之處，Unlike farmyard (不同於農場)。
　　　　(A) 除此之外 (C) 超出之外 (D) 透過，經由
10.　**A**　are dotted 用被動態表示「點綴於或散佈於」。(C) 設立 (D) 覆蓋

句式分析

1 As long as

As long as the weather is warm, there are trailer rides through the Stand Wood forest area.

as/so long as (只要) 是從屬連接詞，常用來表示條件。類似 if、on condition that、provided (that) 的用法。

【例】It doesn't matter who you are, as long as you bring the invitation with you.
　　　➡ It doesn't matter who you are, on condition that you bring the invitation with you.

【例】As long as you are not doing it on purpose, you will be forgiven.
　　　➡ If you are not doing it on purpose, you will be forgiven.

【例】As long as you finish the homework, you can go out to play.
　　　➡ Provided (that) you finish the homework, you can go out to play.

2 S + V + to V : To V, S + V....

You can join a springtime woodland walk to see the wild flowers and newly sprouting trees.

Press the DELETE button again to erase all the messages.

(1) 在以上兩句中不定詞片語表「目的」(join a springtime woodland walk 和 Press the ERASE button)。

(2) 這種不定詞片語表「目的」時，也可放在句首：

【例】 We took various precautions to make our mountain climbing safer.
➡ To make our mountain climbing safer, we took various precautions.

【例】 We got up earlier than usual to attend the conference.
➡ To attend the conference, we got up earlier than usual.

3 S + V + O (N) + to V

Woodland walks are one of the best ways to see these bright autumn colors.

This is a lovely way to enjoy the great English countryside.

不定詞片語放在名詞後面作形容詞修飾。

【例】 We have nothing to worry about.

【例】 Do you have anything to cure a bad cold?

【例】 My daughter needs a bigger box to hold her Barbie dolls.

【例】 I don't think she has anything to be proud of.

【例】 Julie is a nice person to get along with.

問答

1. What is the passage about?

2. In summer what activities can visitors choose to do in the farmland around Chatsworth House?

3. In winter what activities can visitors do in Chatsworth House?

4. What can you find if you walk in the park around Chatsworth House?

 造句

1. as long as

I'll go to the party as long as you are going, too.

_____

2. N + to V

He might be the first government officer to be accused of using his political position for personal enrichment.

_____

3. To V, S + V....

To say goodbye to me, Ally ran after the bus I took.

_____

翻譯

1. 只要你答應不整夜熬夜玩PS3，我就買給你。(as long as...)

I will buy you a PS3 _____

playing with it.

2. 這些孩子需要有人可以和他們談他們的煩惱。

The children need _____ .

3. 我跟我班上大部分人不同，我走路上學。

_____

4. 如果天氣舒適，我們就會到海灘享受和煦微風和陽光。(pleasant, warm breeze)

_____

5. 為了要達到目標，我們必須團結合作。(To V, S + V....)

_____

Pepper Power

Do you like your food spicy? No problem: just sprinkle some pepper on your dish. How easy it is! However, thousands of years ago,   1   food sting on the tongue was not that simple. The black pepper we take for   2   today was unimaginably valuable in ancient times. In fact,   3   it, the world would have been entirely different.

Black pepper comes from the pepper plant. This plant   4   pepper berries. When the fruit is half-ripe, they are dried under the sun until they turn black. After they are   5   to powder, we have the pepper we find on our dining table. This   6   sounds uncomplicated, but years ago black pepper could only be found in India, so it had to travel a long way to get to people who lived in Europe and Africa. This made the spice extremely   7 .

"Black Gold" was   8   black pepper was called before. Black pepper's   9   was so high that peppercorns were found in the nostrils of Egyptian pharaoh Ramesses II's mummy. Furthermore, it is   10   that Attila the Hun would only stop attacking Rome if only the Romans would give him a ton of black pepper. Therefore, it is not surprising that the trade of pepper and other spices between Asia and Europe not only was good business but   11   the discovery of new territory and the establishment of great cities like Venice.

The price of black pepper eventually   12   during the 1600's, when ships could directly and easily go from one continent to another. Now, though pepper certainly isn't expensive, it still has its   13   value. Black pepper is known to be good for one's digestion. The spice tells the   14   to produce a certain acid which breaks down the food we eat. This means food does not stay in our bodies for long. If food   15 , we might have heartburn or indigestion.

UNIT 16

_____ 1. (A) avoiding   (B) preparing   (C) making   (D) preventing

_____ 2. (A) considered   (B) granted   (C) course   (D) instance

_____ 3. (A) with   (B) without   (C) upon   (D) through

_____ 4. (A) exists   (B) holds   (C) falls   (D) grows

_____ 5. (A) ground   (B) grounded   (C) blend   (D) blended

_____ 6. (A) ingredient   (B) formation   (C) process   (D) recipe

_____ 7. (A) edible   (B) practical   (C) precious   (D) ordinary

_____ 8. (A) that   (B) which   (C) of which   (D) what

_____ 9. (A) fame   (B) value   (C) production   (D) consumption

_____ 10. (A) essential   (B) necessary   (C) estimated   (D) rumored

_____ 11. (A) led   (B) led to   (C) resulted   (D) resulted from

_____ 12. (A) went up   (B) went down   (C) raised   (D) soared

_____ 13. (A) medical   (B) market   (C) social   (D) religious

_____ 14. (A) stomach   (B) tongue   (C) liver   (D) lungs

_____ 15. (A) has   (B) is   (C) did   (D) was

NOTE

 原來如此

1. **C** 線索是後面的原形動詞 sting，只有 make 有此用法，make + O + V。
2. **B** take + O + for granted (視…為理所當然)
3. **B** valuable 是線索，既然珍貴，沒有它 (without it) 世界就不同了 (參考句式分析 2)。
4. **D** 植物長出果實，可以用 grow 或 bear。
5. **A** grind something to powder (將…磨成粉)，ground 是過去分詞。
6. **C** 由前兩句得知這是過程 (process)。(A) 成分 (B) 形成 (D) 食譜
7. **C** 因為取得不易，就很珍貴 (precious)。(A) 可吃的 (B) 實用的 (D) 普通的
8. **D** 由句子結構來分析，此格需要的是包含 the thing + which/that 的複合關係代名詞 (參考句式分析 3)。
9. **B** 由 "Black Gold" 和 high 得知，這裡指價值 (value) 高。
   (A) 名聲 (C) 產品 (D) 消費
10. **D** 空格後的敘述並非是「重要或必要」的事。
11. **B** 由空格前後的因果關係得知此格要用「導致」(led to; resulted in)，而非「起因於」(resulted from)。
12. **B** 由空格後的部分得知這是造成價格「下跌」(went down) 的原因，(A)(D) 上漲，(C) 要改為 was raised 或 rose 才正確。
13. **A** 線索在下一句，這是醫學 (medical) 價值。(B) 市場 (C) 社會 (D) 宗教
14. **A** 空格之前的 digestion 和之後的敘述得知此格要選消化器官。
   (B) 舌頭 (C) 肝 (D) 肺
15. **C** 這裡不用助動詞 do 代替前面提過 stay，而用 did (參考句式分析 1)。

句式分析

1 對現在事實提出的假設

If food <u>stayed</u> in our bodies for long, we <u>might have</u> heartburn or indigestion.

在對現在事實提出假設的句子中：
(1) if 條件子句中動詞用過去式；若條件子句中有 be 動詞時，主詞不論任何人稱 be 動詞用 were
(2) 主要子句動詞用 <u>would/might</u> + V
(3) if 條件子句中，不可以使用 would

【例】If Ken were ten years younger, he would consider accepting the job.

【例】The situation would be more complicated if the information were leaked.

2 Without..., S + would + V/have V-en

Without black pepper, the world would have been entirely different.

(1) 在上面這個句子中 Without black pepper (若不是當年有黑胡椒)，有「假設」的含意，因此用法就和假設句相同。

(2) Without black pepper 就可以相當於 If it had not been for black pepper (因為這裡是對過去事實提出假設)，would have been entirely different 是指現在的結果 (世界現在會很不一樣)。但是用 without 句子比較簡潔。

【例】Without computers, what would life be like?

➡ If it were not for computers, what would life be like?

(與現在事實相反用法)

【例】Without his invention, computers would have been much heavier.

➡ If it had not been for his invention, computers would have been much heavier. (與過去事實相反假設用法)

3 what (作複合關係代名詞用法)

"Black Gold" was what black pepper was called before.

what 為複合關係代名詞，本身包含了先行詞，因此它沒有先行詞。語意上等於 the thing(s) that。

【例】**What** (= The thing *that*/*which*) I want to buy is a digital watch.

【例】**What** (= The thing *that*/*which*) Mina does is really mean.

【例】This is **what** (= the thing *that*/*which*) she promised to offer.

【例】Encouragement is **what** (= the thing *that*/*which*) we need now.

其他複合關係代名詞有 whatever、whichever、whoever、whomever。

【例】Do whatever (= anything that) you decide to do.

【例】Take whichever (= any of those that) you like best.

【例】Whoever (= Anyone who) comes first will get the prize.

【例】I'll give it to whoever (= anyone who) comes first.

【例】I'll give it to whomever (= anyone whom) I like.

 問 答

1. What's the main idea of this article?

2. What country is black pepper native to?

3. Why was black pepper valued so highly in ancient Europe?

 造句

1. without
   What would the Lakers do <u>without</u> Kobe Bryant?

   _____

2. take...for granted
   I <u>took</u> it <u>for granted</u> that Mary would offer to pay for the banquet.

   _____

3. go down
   The value of the US dollar has <u>gone down</u> again.

   _____

4. so...that
   The rumor spread <u>so</u> fast <u>that</u> everyone in this town knew about it in half an hour.

   _____

翻譯

1. 謠傳 Whitney Houston 罹患致命的腦瘤。
   It _____ a deadly brain tumor.

2. 我們經常把父母為我們做的事視為當然。(take...for granted)
   We tend to _____.

3. 沒有你財物上的支持，我會是一個徹底的失敗者。
   _____, I would be _____.

4. 十七世紀初期，船舶使人們可以很容易地從一洲到另一洲。
   In the early seventeenth century, ships _____.

5. 這些就是地震的時候你要做的。(what; in case of)

   _____

NOTE

Sleep Need

Have you ever dozed off in class? Have you ever been snapped awake by your teacher angrily calling your name? Have all this been happening to you more and more often? Falling asleep in school may certainly be because of you __1__ late at night or because of your teacher's detailed history lesson. Yet recent studies have shown that other more subtle reasons are at play, and that you are certainly not __2__ off alone.

A __3__ of American teenagers has revealed that only 20% of them get enough sleep. 17% of them have insomnia, which means that the teens cannot get sleep __4__ they want to. There is no __5__ sleep that deprivation haunts many aspects of teenagers' life: it can cause them to feel anxious easily, have low grades at school and a variety of health problems like diabetes, heart disease and obesity. It is __6__ utmost importance that teens get at least nine hours of sleep every night. Then why are many of them having __7__ sleeping at night or keeping awake in the daytime?

There are the usual suspects, of course. Teens __8__ have lots of homework, talk to their friends on the phone and go to many parties—all done till the wee hours of the morning. Researchers are now also pointing at electronic devices as a reason for sleep __9__ . Because cell phones, computers, iPods, and TVs in their rooms __10__ their minds, teenagers have difficulty finding downtime. What's more, when teens hit puberty, melatonin—a hormone that helps people sleep—gets released at around one in the morning. This means teenagers can't get __11__ soon enough, which thus results in lack of sleep.

So how can teens reclaim lost hours of sleep? Perhaps they can do so __12__ exercising during the daytime, getting ready for bed at the same time every day, and __13__ all electronics off before bedtime so everything is relaxed and quiet.

_____ 1. (A) lay over   (B) sit up   (C) staying up   (D) leaving out

_____ 2. (A) laying   (B) taking   (C) setting   (D) nodding

_____ 3. (A) survey   (B) suspect   (C) routine   (D) project

_____ 4. (A) even   (B) especially   (C) even so   (D) even if

_____ 5. (A) way   (B) doubt   (C) knowing   (D) predicting

_____ 6. (A) at   (B) to   (C) of   (D) in

_____ 7. (A) capacity   (B) trouble   (C) expectation   (D) possibility

_____ 8. (A) easy to   (B) apt to   (C) tend to   (D) intend to

_____ 9. (A) efficiency   (B) deficiency   (C) sufficiency   (D) frequency

_____ 10. (A) overcome   (B) overlook   (C) overstimulate   (D) overemphasize

_____ 11. (A) sleepy   (B) awake   (C) confused   (D) refreshed

_____ 12. (A) in   (B) to   (C) on   (D) by

_____ 13. (A) turning   (B) running   (C) shut   (D) throw

NOTE

*Cloze Writing &
Practice*

原來如此

1. **C** 注意空格前的 you (此處是受格) 也有人在此位置用 your。還要注意之前的 because of，造成此格要用 V-ing。sit up 或 stay up 都是熬夜。

2. **D** 第一句 doze off (打瞌睡) 是很好的線索。研究指出你不是唯一 nod off (打瞌睡) 的人。

3. **A** (A) 調查報告 (B) 懷疑 (C) 例行公事 (D) 策劃

4. **D** 由句構判斷這個空格需要從屬連接詞 even if (即使)，而 even (甚至) 則是副詞 (參考句式分析 1)。

5. **B** 這一句承接上兩句，更進一步指出：青少年睡眠缺乏無疑地 (there is no doubt that)。There is no + knowing that.... ➜ It is impossible to know that....

6. **C** of + 抽象名詞相當於 Adj. 用法。of importance = important

7. **B** have difficulty/trouble 之後要接 V-ing (參考句式分析 2)。

8. **C** tend (v.) (容易，有…傾向)，easy 和 apt 有類似字義，但都是 Adj.。

9. **B** 由上文得知此篇談的是青少年睡眠不足的問題。
   (A) 效率 (B) 缺乏 (C) 足夠 (D) 頻率

10. **C** (A) 克服 (B) 忽視 (C) 過度刺激 (D) 過度強調

11. **A** 上一句得知它們不會這麼早有睡意 (sleepy)。

12. **D** by + V-ing (動名詞) 用來表達方法 (參考句式分析 3)。

13. **A** 由 exercising..., getting..., and 得知這是 A, B, and C 的連接，空格當然也要用 V-ing，而關上電子產品就用 turning off，(C) 選項若改為 shutting 就正確了。

句式分析

1 even if

The teens cannot get sleep <u>even if</u> they want to.

(1) even (*adv.*) 用來加強 if 子句
   【例】People should be able to respect others <u>even if</u> they're rich and important.
   【例】<u>Even if</u> it rains tomorrow, the outing will not be cancelled.
   【例】I really want to have a Wii (the new video game console) <u>even if</u> I have to queue up for days.

(2) even if 也可以用來表達「與現在事實相反」的假設用法。

【例】 Even if you gave me one billion dollars, I would not take the job.

【例】 Stella would not give up her dream even if she failed in the end.

2 have trouble/difficulty + V-ing

Why are many of them having trouble **sleeping** or **keeping** awake?

Because cell phones, computers, iPods, and TVs in their rooms overstimulate their minds, teenagers have difficulty **finding** downtime.

have difficulty/trouble (有困難) 之後要接 V-ing (動名詞)。

【例】 We have great difficulty **finding** a new team member.

【例】 Adam had trouble **using** the mouse because his pointing finger got hurt.

【例】 Slow readers have difficulty **trying** to catch up.

【例】 The old lady has trouble **reading** the sign on the sliding door of the MRT station.

3 by + V-ing

Perhaps they can do so **by** exercising during the daytime, getting ready for bed at the same time every day, and turning all electronics off before bedtime so everything is relaxed and quiet.

by + V-ing (動名詞) 用來表達藉由某種方法，例如下面的例句中 closing her eyes 就是 fought off the dizziness 的方法

【例】 Sue fought off the dizziness **by** closing her eyes.

【例】 Please support our work **by** making a donation.

【例】 Mr. Mason leads his life **by** selling household goods.

問 答

1. What's the main idea of this article?

2. How many aspects of teenagers' life may be affected by the lack of sleep?

3. Do you have difficulty keeping awake in class? Why?

改寫句子

1. The young man designs webpages. As a result, he makes his own living.
   (以 by + V-ing 改寫成一句)

   _____

2. Homeworking is a growing trend. I am absolutely certain of that.
   (以 there is no doubt that 改寫成一句)

   _____

3. It is very difficult for patients to pay for expensive medical treatments.
   (以 have difficulty 改寫)

   _____

   _____

翻譯

1. 我們可以從瞭解我們都市從何處取得水以及如何處理水，來開始關心水的問題。
   (by + V-ing)
   We can begin to care about water problems _____
   _____ and _____ .

2. 印度菜現在名列世界上最有特色的菜餚之一，這是毫無疑問的。
   _____ now ranks among the most distinctive
   cuisines of the world.

3. 他很難解釋為什麼選擇留下 (have difficulty)。
   _____ he chose to stay.

4. 即使你試著逃避現實，情況還是惡化。

   _____

5. 我祖母很容易在看電視的時候打瞌睡。

   _____

NOTE

ORBIS in Taiwan

ORBIS is an international non-profit non-governmental organization. It offers free medical treatment and training for the __1__ of blindness and is best known for its "Flying Eye Hospital," a modified DC-10 aircraft. ORBIS not only has its headquarters in New York, __2__ has offices in Houston, London, Hong Kong, and Taipei.

Taiwan was __3__ as ORBIS' second Asian office because of Taiwan's high standard of ophthalmology and economic achievements. In 2001, ORBIS Taiwan was registered as an international non-governmental development organization.

__4__ in Taipei, ORBIS Taiwan is headed by Managing Director Dr. Tsai, a professor in the Department of Ophthalmology at Taipei Medical University. __5__ his direction, ORBIS Taiwan's mission includes conducting eye care education programs for local school children, __6__ vision healthcare activities for local and overseas communities, and supporting ORBIS International programs.

Among its many activities, in July 2005, ORBIS Taiwan volunteers flew to Xinjiang in mainland China __7__ a week-long pediatric ophthalmology training and free treatment program. __8__ the strong sunshine in Xinjiang, many people suffer from glaucoma (青光眼) and cataracts (白內障); however, because of the poor economic conditions there, many families cannot afford proper treatment. The ORBIS Taiwan program thus __9__ many.

One of the cases that ORBIS Taiwan doctors saw __10__ a five-year-old boy named Muladeger. He suffered from glaucoma since birth but was lucky enough __11__ a free operation from ORBIS America in 2001, which saved his right eye. During this program, ORBIS Taiwan doctors __12__ the vision in his left eye, and now he can see clearly.

ORBIS Taiwan has been able to continue its operations with funding from ORBIS International and __13__ from local banks, corporations, clubs, and private individuals. However, ORBIS Taiwan still has an ongoing __14__ to raise awareness and money to help the __15__ to eliminate unnecessary blindness. More can be done to keep the "Flying Eye Hospital" flying.

_____ 1. (A) precaution   (B) creation   (C) production   (D) prevention

_____ 2. (A) and   (B) but   (C) then   (D) thus

_____ 3. (A) regarded   (B) thought   (C) selected   (D) despised

_____ 4. (A) Based   (B) Found   (C) Situating   (D) Spotting

_____ 5. (A) In   (B) On   (C) Under   (D) Beyond

_____ 6. (A) took part   (B) taking part   (C) carried out   (D) carrying out

_____ 7. (A) organizing   (B) receiving   (C) to conduct   (D) to undergo

_____ 8. (A) Except for   (B) Due to   (C) Because   (D) As

_____ 9. (A) favored   (B) approved   (C) honored   (D) benefited

_____ 10. (A) do   (B) does   (C) was   (D) is

_____ 11. (A) to receive   (B) to reject   (C) to perform   (D) to undertake

_____ 12. (A) distracted   (B) impaired   (C) destroyed   (D) restored

_____ 13. (A) citizenship   (B) sponsorship   (C) membership   (D) scholarship

_____ 14. (A) organization   (B) organism   (C) campaign   (D) companion

_____ 15. (A) fight   (B) opposition   (C) protest   (D) dispute

原來如此

1. **D** 由本句和下文文意得知此機構的任務之一是預防失明。
2. **B** 前有 not only 所以此格選 but。
3. **C** selected (選擇)，因為高水準的眼科醫學和經濟成就而被選為…。(D) 鄙視
4. **A** based... (根據地在台北) 為分詞片語修飾 ORBIS Taiwan。
5. **C** under one's direction (在…的指導之下)。
6. **D** 與 conducting... 和 supporting... 都是 includes 的受詞，故此格應選擇同形的動詞，carry out (達成 / 完成)，take part in... (參加)。
7. **C** to conduct (進行)，不定詞表達 flew to... 的目的。undergo an operation (接受手術)。
8. **B** due to (由於)，because 和 as 是從屬連接詞之後要接子句。
9. **D** benefit (使…獲益)。(A) 表示好感 (B) 贊成 (C) 嘉許、給予榮耀
10. **C** 主動詞倒序，主詞是 boy，而且是指過去的事要用過去式 was。
11. **A** receive an operation (接受手術)，perform (施行)。(D) 擔負
12. **D** restored... (恢復)。(A) 使…分散 (B) 傷害 (C) 毀壞
13. **B** sponsorship (贊助)。(A) 公民身份 (B) 會員身份 (C) 獎學金
14. **C** raise money (募款)，這類活動是 campaign。(A) 組織 (B) 有機體 (D) 同伴
15. **A** fight (奮戰)。(B) 反對 (C) 抗議 (D) 爭論

句式分析

1 adj./adv. + enough + to -V

He was <u>lucky enough to receive</u> a free operation from ORBIS America in 2001 that saved his right eye.

The car designed by the team cannot run <u>fast enough to maintain</u> highway speed.

adj./adv. + enough + to-V (此類用法的不定詞片語表結果)

【例】Bill did not run <u>quickly enough to catch</u> the bus.

【例】Is the weather <u>good enough to have</u> a picnic in the park?

【例】I don't think it is <u>warm enough to swim</u> outdoors.

【例】Lily is now <u>strong enough to live</u> without Jason's company.

【例】Remember that your child is not <u>old enough to be</u> home alone.

2 Due to

Due to the strong sunshine in Xinjiang, many people suffer from glaucoma and cataracts.

Due to poor eating habits, including overeating and skipping meals, poor nutrition among teenagers is on the rise.

(1) **due to** (由於，因…而起) 是介詞的用法，之後要接名詞做為受詞。

【例】Due to/Because of/Owing to supply shortages, we are unable to offer this product from now on.

【例】Poor nutrition among teenagers is on the rise due to/because of/owing to poor eating habits, including overeating and skipping meals.

(2) 另外一種用法 due to 出現在 be 動詞之後，例如：

【例】It is said that the car accident last night **was** due to/because of drunken driving.

【例】The power failure **was** due to/because of a lightning strike.

 問 答

1. What's the main idea of this passage?

2. Why was Taiwan selected as ORBIS' second Asian office?

3. Why do people in Xinjiang easily have eye diseases, such as glaucoma and cataracts?

 造 句

1. enough to-V

How many people are lucky <u>enough to love</u> what they do?

2. to suffer from

Millions of Americans <u>suffer from</u> loss of sleep, but may not realize it.

3. Due to

<u>Due to</u> humidity and heat, we felt exhausted after a long walk in the park.

UNIT 18

翻譯

1. 要記住你的孩子年齡還不夠大到可以獨自留在家裡。

   Remember that _____ .

2. 由於成長快速，年輕孩子需要足夠的營養。

   _____, young children _____ .

3. 這機構不僅提供患眼疾的人免費醫療，而且讓許多眼科醫師受惠。

   The organization _____ with eye diseases

   but also _____ .

4. 為了幫助需要幫助的人，我們發起募款活動。

   _____, we organize a _____

   _____ .

5. 這間豪宅最出名的是它收藏的現代雕塑。(best known)

   The mansion _____ of modern sculptures.

Nutrients & Uniforms

A. 文意選填：由下列單字中選最適當者填入空格中 (請注意大小寫)

only	the other	with	without	forms
however	therefore	another	build	single

Nutrients working with other nutrients make the difference in our health and well-being. No (1) _____ nutrient can work properly alone. For example, it takes calcium to (2) _____ strong bones, but that is (3) _____ the beginning. Without vitamin D, the calcium cannot be taken into the body. The use of protein is (4) _____ example. Protein (5) _____ part of every cell and all the fluids that travel in and around the cells. (6) _____, it takes vitamin C to help make the fluids between the cells. (7) _____ vitamin C, the protein cannot do its job.

B. 文意選填：由下列單字中選最適當者填入空格中 (請注意大小寫)

suit	taste	as	like	lastly
are	is	moreover	firstly	tell

Most students don't agree with school uniforms for three reasons.
(8) _____, when you have to wear the same clothes as everyone else does, you don't have a chance to develop your personal (9) _____ in the way you dress.
(10) _____, people who look scruffy usually look scruffy in their uniforms too and you can always (11) _____ who come from poor family because their uniforms are not (12) _____ new or don't fit properly. (13) _____, the main reason why most students don't like school uniforms (14) _____ because most schools choose such horrible colors and styles that don't (15) _____ young people at all.

原來如此

1.	**single**	由上一句得知此格要選 single，沒有一種營養品可以單獨產生作用。
2.	**build**	build strong bones 形成強壯的骨骼。
3.	**only**	由下一句得知，沒有鈣不能對骨骼有幫助，因此攝取鈣質只是開端。
4.	**another**	由第三句的 for example 得知那是第一個 example，因此選 another 表示還有其他例子。不選 the other 是因為之前沒有指出只有兩個。
5.	**forms**	蛋白質形成部分的細胞。
6.	**However**	由前後語意轉折得知。therefore 因此。
7.	**Without**	without 和 cannot 搭配是指不能沒有…。由上一句得知 protein 一定要配合 vitamin C 才能產生作用。
8.	**Firstly**	常用在列舉時的第一項。
9.	**taste**	taste in the way you dress 衣著品味。
10.	**Moreover**	表示除了前者之外還有後者。
11.	**tell**	在本句中 tell 的字意是「辨別」。
12.	**as**	此處的 not as new 是 not as new as other people's uniforms 的省略。
13.	**Lastly**	常用在列舉時的最後一項。
14.	**is**	主詞是 the main reason，是單數形，所以動詞用 is。
15.	**suit**	顏色和款式不適合年輕人。

寫作要點

段落結構的寫作要領 (一)

1 認識段落

段落是由一群表達某一個「中心思想」的句子所組成，它是整篇作文的一部分，本身就是一個完整的單位。

段落結構的三個部分

(1) 主題句 (Topic Sentence)：

是表達全段中心思想的句子，通常出現在第一句，也可在段落中間或結尾處。其目的可以清楚地告訴讀者本段的中心思想，主題句出現在第一句，在寫作時可以時時提醒作者勿偏離此中心思想。

(2) 支持句 (Supporting Sentences)：

是段落的「主體」。它的功能是支持、說明、闡述、申論主題句。這些句子充分擴展了中心思想。

(3) 結論句 (Concluding Sentence)：

通常出現在段落結尾處，將主題句及討論部分的支持論點做個歸納或總結，此部分有時是省略的。

2 段落範例

Don't mistake knowledge for wisdom. No matter how much information or knowledge you have accumulated, you'll never make sound judgments if you don't have wisdom. Wisdom comes from imagination and reflection. If you can imagine the possible future outcomes of your present decisions and actions, you can avoid mistakes. And if you can reflect on the mistakes you have made, you can avoid making mistakes again and again. Such is wisdom.

（取自八十六年度大學入學考試閱讀測驗試題）

結構分析如下

Topic Sentence: Don't mistake knowledge for wisdom.

Supporting Sentences:

Point 1: Information or knowledge is not wisdom.

Point 2: Wisdom comes from imagination and reflection.

Concluding Sentence: Such is wisdom.

 寫作練習

A. 由四個選項中選出最適當的句子填入空格內，成為段落的主題句。

1. ＿＿＿＿＿＿＿＿＿＿＿＿＿＿＿＿＿＿＿＿＿＿＿＿＿＿＿＿＿＿

You may skip breakfast to get to school or work on time. Sometimes, you may not have time for a good lunch. It may seem easy to fill up on potato chips and candy bars from a snack machine. However, you may find yourself feeling tired on these days. Often you are unable to think clearly. It is hard to pay attention to studies. These signs are telling you to take time to eat correctly.

(A) It's important to pay attention to studies.

(B) It's necessary to eat the right foods.

(C) It's easy to slip into bad eating habits.

(D) It's easy to form eating habits.

2. _____

The dairy group has foods like milk, cheese, and yogurt. The other three groups are the meat and fish group, the fruit and vegetable group, and the bread group. Each meal should have at least one food from the four basic groups. The right combination of these foods will give you needed energy during the day.

(A) A well-balanced diet supports our body's normal growth and development.
(B) To achieve a balanced diet, you can start with the four food groups.
(C) There are four guidelines available to help people plan their balanced diet.
(D) The key to a healthy lifestyle is following a balanced diet.

B. 詳讀以下段落之後寫出主題句。

1. _____

Scientists in Japan studied the hearing of 150 high school students who used headphones regularly. They found that eight students had a hearing loss. These eight students listened to their stereo headphones an average of six hours a day. But when they stopped using the headphones, their hearing returned to normal.

2. _____

When you're doing it, you may notice you're breathing faster than normal. Aerobic exercise can get your heart pumping, make you sweat, and quicken your breathing. If you give your heart this kind of exercise on a regular basis, your heart will get even better at its main job.

Technology and Education

Recent developments in technology have changed our educational system. One obvious __1__ on students today has been television. Young children start watching educational programs, such as Sesame Street, from the age of one or two. These programs are designed to __2__ children while introducing them to numbers, letters, and simple math. For elementary and __3__ students, there are after-school programs about math, science, and reading. Some universities offer __4__ for TV classes. Students can go to a classroom and watch a professor lecturing on television, or they can watch specially-__5__ programs at home.

Another big influence on education has been the personal computer, which is becoming an increasingly important educational __6__. There are many software programs __7__ on every school subject and topic from __8__ to adult level. Students enjoy using computers because they can work by themselves and __9__ their own pace. Many software programs are designed as games. These programs are popular because they are entertaining and educational __10__. In addition, many students use computers to get information from __11__ services and the Internet, and use word-processing programs to do their assignments. With the __12__ in modern technology, the tools students use have evolved.

1.	(A) affect	(B) influence	(C) consequence	(D) factor
2.	(A) tease	(B) threaten	(C) entertain	(D) effect
3.	(A) secondary	(B) secondly	(C) high	(D) college
4.	(A) fines	(B) bonuses	(C) penalties	(D) credits
5.	(A) designing	(B) designed	(C) design	(D) designer
6.	(A) method	(B) technique	(C) tool	(D) system
7.	(A) basic	(B) elementary	(C) recreational	(D) available
8.	(A) after-school	(B) in-class	(C) pre-school	(D) grown-up
9.	(A) to	(B) on	(C) at	(D) with
10.	(A) at the same time	(B) for the time being	(C) on the contrary	(D) on the other hand
11.	(A) in a line	(B) line up	(C) off-line	(D) on-line
12.	(A) change	(B) advance	(C) experiment	(D) breakup

原來如此

1. **B** 對學生有影響 (influence) 的是電視，介系詞 on 也可視為線索。
   (A) 影響 (C) 結果 (D) 因素

2. **C** entertain (*v.t.*) 娛樂，使有趣。節目設計的目的是教學的同時也娛樂小朋友。
   (A) 取笑 (B) 威脅 (D) 引起

3. **A** 由之前的「初等教育的」(elementary) 得知此格選「中等教育的」(secondary)。

4. **D** (A) 罰款 (B) 紅利獎金 (C) 刑罰，懲罰 (D) 學分

5. **B** 複合形容詞的結構是 Adv. + V-en 或 Adv. + V-ing，選擇過去分詞或現在分詞則由動詞和後面的名詞之間的關係決定。此處 the program is specially designed 是被動關係，因此用過去分詞構成 specially-designed program。如果是 the car is moving fast，就構成 fast-moving car。

6. **C** 電腦是一種主要的教育工具 (tool)。(A) 方法 (B) 技巧 (D) 系統，制度

7. **D** 由本句文意得知可以得到每一個學科每一種程度適用的軟體。 available (*adj.*) 可使用的，可得到的，修飾 programs。
   (A) 基本的 (B) 初步的 (C) 娛樂的

8. **C** pre-school (學齡前的)。此句為 from pre-school level to adult level 的省略。

9. **C** at one's own pace 以自己的步調。

10. **A** 同時具有娛樂性和教育性，at the same time 同時。
    (B) 暫時 (C) 相反地 (D) 另一方面

11. **D** on-line(連線的，線上的)，由之後的 the Internet 可以得知此格選填 on-line。
    (A) 成排，成列 (B) 排隊 (C) 離線

12. **B** 由之後的 evolve (進展，進步) 及本篇短文第一行 developments in technology 得知此處是指「科技的進步」。(B) 進步 (C) 實驗 (D) 中斷

寫作要點

段落結構的寫作要領 (二)

如何發展段落：

寫好了主題句之後，下一步就要根據主題句列出支持句部分的要點，根據這些要點發展成段落。

A. 要點的安排一定要有次序 (**order or sequence**)。

有次序才能有條理。次序可以是時間的次序、空間的次序或重要性的次序，例如：從早到晚，從現在到過去、從遠到近或從近到遠，從不重要到重要。例如本單元克漏字文章第一段安排電視的影響的次序就是：「兩三歲→小學中學→大學，從年幼至長」。

B. 支持句部分中的句子都必須比主題句明確 (**specific**)，才能充分地闡明主題。

段落中的句子都要遵循著從籠統 (**general**) 到明確 (**specific**) 的規則。例如：

A certain amount of stress is actually necessary for survival. It provides the body's survival mechanism. A stress reaction can sometimes save a person's life by releasing hormones that enable a person to react quickly and with greater energy in a dangerous situation. (第一句 necessary for survival 是最 general 的表達，第二句用了比較 specific 的 survival mechanism，第三句則是提出細節說明這種機制，當然是最 specific 的句子。)

C. 支持句 (即段落發展) 經常運用的方式：

(a) 舉例說明 (**examples**)：常用「轉折語」有 for example、for instance。

(b) 列舉 (**listing**)：常用「時間順序」的轉折語有 first、second、last、next …等。

(c) 提出理由 (**reasons**) 或解釋 (**explanation**)：依「重要順序」排列說明。

(d) 細節 (**details**)

(e) 比較 (**comparison**) 或對照 (**contrast**)：常用有 likewise、similarly、on the contrary、in contrast …等。

(f) 提出統計數字 (**statistics**) 或研究結果

這些方式有時單獨使用，有時也可以合併使用。例如：

1. Water or other liquids are not the only source of fluids. Foods, like fruits and vegetables, are also important sources. For example, a turkey sandwich made with Swiss cheese, lettuce, and tomato on whole-wheat bread contains almost a half-cup of water. (以舉例來說明)
2. Most cities today regulate the disposal of garbage. First, they have chemical treatment plants which convert garbage to fertilizer. Second, they use treated garbage to fill in land. A third way of disposal is to set up incineration plants for burning garbage. (以列舉的方式提出說明)
3. Why do friends matter? There is a simple reason why they matter. As humans, we were designed to be social beings because we can do far more together to improve one another's lives than we can in isolation. We need friends not just for survival, but for comfort and closeness that money can't buy. (以理由說明)

4. All farm workers are some of the most exploited people in this country. They work from dawn to dusk, often with no breaks in the heat of the day. Workers go out into fields that are often still wet with pesticides. Unable to wash, they are forced to eat with the pesticides on their hands.
(第二句以後詳述工人受到剝削的細節來說明)

5. A survey of American teenagers has revealed that only 20% of them get enough sleep. 17% of them have insomnia, which means that the teens cannot get sleep even if they want to. There is no doubt sleep deprivation haunts many aspects of teenagers' life: it can cause them to feel anxious have low grades and a variety of health problems like diabetes, heart disease, and obesity. It is of utmost importance that teens get at least nine hours of sleep every night. Then why are many of them having trouble sleeping at night or keeping awake in the daytime? (以統計數字及研究結果來說明)

D. 結論句的寫法：

(1) 結論句最常見的方式是回到主題，也就是用不同的文字重述主題句。

例如，主題句是 "Trekking in high mountains is very dangerous, so we must be well-prepared."。

結論句是 "Making good preparations is the key to safe trekking."

(2) 另外一種常見的方式是將段落做結論，例如，主題句是 "Don't mistake knowledge for wisdom."。經過一段論述之後，結論句是 "Such is wisdom."。

 寫作練習

A. 請根據以下的主題句及要點擴展成一個段落

Topic Sentence: My two uncles Tom and John are similar in many ways.

    Point 1: appearance

    Point 2: job

    Point 3: love for their nieces and nephews

B. 請以下列主題句自行擬定要點，擴展成一個段落

(1) My senior high school days are full of laughter and warmth.

(2) Iris and I are twins but we are different in many ways.

(3) I (don't) like the summer for three reasons.

 **參考範例**

A. My two uncles Tom and John are similar in many ways. They look and act so much alike that some people think that they are twins. They are both of medium height and have broad shoulders. Both of them are going bald in their early thirties. Tom, a PE teacher, likes to be with teenagers. He teaches them to play basketball. John teaches English in a senior high school and is a good tennis player. He is enthusiastic about teaching his colleagues to play tennis. They often stay outdoors, so they both have a dark complexion. What's more, they love their nieces and nephews very much. Every time they hear us call "Uncle Tom" or "Uncle John," they smile radiantly right away and give us a big hug. They are really good uncles and good teachers.

B (1) My senior high school days are full of laughter and warmth. Friendship makes me feel warm. When I get good grades or win any prize, I share the joy with my classmates. When I fail my exams, they are just there to encourage me. When I get stuck in any math problems, they help me solve them. Friendship always gives me strength and faith to cope with frustrations. With friendship, I am still happy in spite of the heavy school load.

A Newspaper Article

Today a jury of seven men and five women said that 78-year-old Mr. Andrew Mullins was guilty of murdering his 80-year-old wife, Edith. Six weeks ago, Mullins ___1___ on trial for murder.

The tragedy happened on the night of August 10th in Mr. and Mrs. Mullins' home in the small town of Palmston Beach. That morning Mullins' wife, who had ___2___ from lung cancer and Alzheimer's disease, looked at him ___3___ empty eyes and asked, "Who are you?" That evening she was ___4___ and kept saying, "Help me, help me." As she slept on the sofa that night, Mullins put a gun against her head and ___5___ her. Then he telephoned the police and told them what he had done. The police came to the house and arrested him. It was two days later that he was ___6___ with murder.

During the trial Mullins said, "The woman I killed was not my wife. It was a body in pain and a mind with no memory. I don't think I ___7___ the murder."

Several witnesses were called to give ___8___. Some of their neighbors said that Mrs. Mullins liked to go out, and that she always smiled and wore make-up. The doctors said that Mrs. Mullins was extremely seriously ill. Their friends said that Mr. Mullins loved his wife very much. But in the end the jury ___9___ a verdict of guilty. They agreed with the prosecutor. It was murder.

Tomorrow the judge will pass sentence. The law says he must send Mullins to ___10___ for at least twenty-five years. That means he will not be released from prison until he is 103 years old.

_____ 1. (A) stood   (B) laid   (C) went   (D) relied

_____ 2. (A) healed   (B) treated   (C) cured   (D) suffered

_____ 3. (A) with   (B) in   (C) on   (D) of

_____ 4. (A) in great joy   (B) in terrible pain   (C) delighted   (D) shocked

_____ 5. (A) shot   (B) shot at   (C) fired   (D) fired at

_____ 6. (A) accused   (B) sentenced   (C) convinced   (D) charged

_____ 7. (A) prevented   (B) committed   (C) performed   (D) managed

_____ 8. (A) hypothesis   (B) supposition   (C) evidence   (D) trial

_____ 9. (A) remained   (B) reached   (C) came   (D) arrived

_____ 10. (A) jail   (B) the jail   (C) imprison   (D) the prison

UNIT 21

NOTE

原來如此

1. **C** go on trial 接受審判。
2. **D** suffer from... 罹患 (某病)。(A) 癒合 (B) 治療，處理 (C) 治癒
3. **A** with empty eyes 以空洞的眼光
4. **B** 由前文她患病得知此題選 in terrible pain (非常痛苦)。
        (A) 非常喜悅 (C) 歡喜的 (D) 震驚的
5. **A** (A) 槍殺某人 (B) 指瞄準某人射擊 (C) 開除某人 (D) 對某人射擊。
6. **D** (A) 指控 (B) 判刑 (C) 說服
7. **B** commit a crime/murder 犯罪。(A) 避免 (C) 實施，履行，演出 (D) 經營管理
8. **C** 證人 (witness) 提供證據 (give evidence)。(A) 假設 (B) 假定 (D) 審判
9. **B** reach a verdict 達成判決
10. **A** be sent to jail/prison 被送進監獄，在此片語中 jail 及 prison 之前不加定冠詞 the。(C) 監禁 (v.)

寫作要點

摘要寫作

A. 什麼是摘要？

在高中階段最常見的是老師會要求你把寒暑假作業讀的一本故事書、一篇文章、課文內容、或一篇新聞報導寫出摘要，以測試你對內容瞭解的程度。摘要寫作是很好的寫作練習，寫作的過程還可以幫助你更瞭解閱讀的內容。

B. 為何要練習摘要寫作？

摘要是以簡潔 (concise) 而清楚 (clear) 的，而且<u>不同於原作者使用的文字重述原作者</u>的作品。

C. 如何寫摘要？

原則：

(1) 比原文短，大約三分之一的長度 (也有老師要求你只寫三五句的)。

(2) 必須包含原文的主旨 (main idea) 及支持句 (supporting sentences) 的要點 (points)，不包含要點中的細節。

(3) 不可抄襲原文，只能<u>用自己的文字</u>。更<u>不可加入自己的意見或想法</u>。

(4) 摘要和文章一樣要點的安排必須有邏輯次序 (logical order)。

步驟：

(1) 仔細閱讀文章，充分了解內容。

(2) 找出文章的主旨及支持句的要點。

(3) 根據主旨和要點列出大綱 (outline)。

(4) 根據大綱用自己的文字將文章大意簡潔扼要的寫出來。

※如果是一則故事就要另外注意 a. 故事的主要人物 b. 故事中的主要情節發生在何時何地 c. 按照它們發生的時間順序，寫下故事。

※如果是一則新聞報導，一開始就要說明來源，例如：

> According to a July 21, 2005 news article in the *USA TODAY*, "*It's written all over your face*," the seven basic emotions — anger, contempt, disgust, fear, happiness, sadness and surprise—have clear facial signals.

 寫作練習

A. 以本篇克漏字短文練習摘要寫作。仔細閱讀短文後，回答下列問題，然後加入適當的承轉語 (transitional words)，成為一段，就是摘要。

(1) How old was Mrs. Mullins?

(2) What disease had she suffered from for several years?

(3) How did the tragedy happen?

(4) After that what did he do?

(5) Was he arrested?

(6) Did he think that he committed a crime? Why?

(7) What did the jury think of the tragedy?

(8) How many years will he be sentenced to in prison?

B. 下面是 Unit 20 中的克漏字文章的大綱，再一次詳讀這篇文章之後，根據這個大綱寫出摘要：

Main Idea: Developments in technology have changed our educational system.

Supporting Sentences:

    Point 1: television (young children; elementary and secondary students; college students)

    Point 2: personal computer (software programs; Internet and word processors)

C. 仔細閱讀 Unit 10 有關鐵達尼號的報導，然後寫出它的摘要。

D. 以 50 個字寫出你最近讀的故事書或看的電影情節的摘要。

E. 以 3–4 個句子（大約 40 個字）寫出下列這段文字的摘要。

In the summer of 1853, potato chip recipe was created by an American chef named George Crum at Moon Lake Lodge in Saratoga Springs, New York. One dinner guest found Crum's fried potatoes too thick for his liking and sent them back. Crum sliced and fried some thinner ones, but these were also not thin enough. Losing his temper, the chef decided to annoy the guest by slicing and frying the potatoes so thin and crisp that they couldn't be eaten with a fork. He was sure the complainer would leave, after being unable to cut these ridiculous fries with his fork. Yet the man was delighted with them, and other guests began ordering the same delicious snack. The potato chip was born and soon became popular throughout New England.

 參考範例

A. Summary

Mrs. Mullins, 80 years old, had suffered from lung cancer and Alzheimer's disease. One night in their home, she felt great pain and she kept on asking her husband to help her. So he did help her, but by shooting her. Then he called the police and was arrested. He didn't think that he committed a crime because he thought he just killed a body in pain and a mind with no memory. But the jury agreed that it was murder. He will be sentenced to at least 25 years in prison.

C. Summary

On April 10th, 1912, the *Titanic*, which was considered to be unsinkable, left from Southampton to sail for New York. It was her first voyage. Four days later, while crossing the icy waters of the North Atlantic, she hit an iceberg in spite of the fact that she had tried to turn sharply to avoid colliding with the iceberg. When the captain went down to see how she had been damaged, he realized that the *Titanic* was going to be lost, because she was sinking very rapidly. He immediately gave an order to abandon the ship. Because there were not enough lifeboats for all the passengers, 1,500 people had to stay behind and were finally drowned.

Ancient China Comes to the U.S.

The ancient Chinese art of Feng Shui has come to the United States! Feng Shui is the way of arranging houses, offices and furniture __1__ harmony with nature. Fans believe that Feng Shui can help bring us health, wealth and happiness. Americans have embraced Feng Shui __2__ a lot of enthusiasm—it's now possible to buy books about Feng Shui in English from almost every bookstore. There are also websites and even colleges in America __3__ to the teaching of Feng Shui.

Why is Feng Shui so popular in the US? Well, many Americans live in crowded, busy cities a long way from nature, and have fast-__4__ lives. Feng Shui is a way for them to __5__ their homes more peaceful and __6__ with the environment. They believe that homes and offices with good Feng Shui are more relaxing.

Feng Shui is practical for anyone. Think of the desk __7__ you do most of your study. Is it __8__, with food containers, books and papers lying everywhere? Or is it tidy and clean, with your pens and pencils neatly __9__. An orderly desk is a good way to start, while Feng Shui is more complicated than these tricks . Now, why not organize your workplace to __10__ your working efficiency in a Feng Shui way?

_____ 1. (A) to destroy   (B) to create   (C) maintaining   (D) establishing
_____ 2. (A) with   (B) in   (C) to   (D) of
_____ 3. (A) are devoted   (B) which devotes (C) devoting   (D) devoted
_____ 4. (A) pacing   (B) paced   (C) growing   (D) grown
_____ 5. (A) cause   (B) make   (C) let   (D) tend
_____ 6. (A) in touch   (B) in company   (C) in action   (D) in line
_____ 7. (A) that   (B) which   (C) where   (D) how
_____ 8. (A) comfortable   (B) cozy   (C) messy   (D) spacious
_____ 9. (A) to arrange   (B) to be arranged (C) arranged   (D) arranging
_____ 10. (A) enhance   (B) decrease   (C) build   (D) lower

原來如此

1. **B** 此格用不定詞表示 arranging... 的目的，由下文得知風水是創造 (to create) 而非破壞 (to destroy) 和諧。

2. **A** with enthusiasm 相當於 enthusiastically，以副詞來修飾動詞 (embrace)。

3. **D** 此格可以用關係子句 which are devoted 或省略關係代名詞與動詞，以過去分詞 devoted 修飾 websites and colleges。

4. **B** 「複合形容詞」有一類是 **Adj. + N-ed**: fast-paced (步調快的)，bad-tempered (壞脾氣的)，fast-growing (成長快速的)。

5. **B** peaceful 是線索，此格選可以用形容詞當受詞補語的動詞 make。

6. **D** 由第一段的 harmony 得知風水是與環境和諧，in line with (與…一致)。

7. **C** 空格之後的句子結構中 (主詞 you，動詞 do，受詞 most of your study) 都已經完整，所以此空格不選關係代名詞，而選關係副詞，where= at which。

8. **C** with...lying everywhere 是線索，東西散落各處當然是 messy (雜亂)。

9. **C** 這是 with 片語的用法 (見 Unit 8 句式分析 1)。

10. **A** 由 working efficiency 可推測，以風水的角度來「提升」工作效率。

寫作要點

統一性與連貫性

除了之前介紹的 topic sentence 和 supporting sentences 之外，要寫出好的段落或文章還要認識其他兩個要素：A. 統一性 (Unity)　　B. 連貫性 (Coherence and Cohesion)。

A. 統一性 (Unity)

統一性就是段落主題的單一性。段落只表達一個中心思想，每一個句子必須支持段落主題，不得偏離。要達到統一性就要遵守以下原則：段落中不能有和主題不相干的陳述。

> Astronauts often work 16 hours a day on the space shuttle in order to complete all the projects set out for the mission. The space shuttle is launched vertically, carrying usually five to seven astronauts into space. From space, astronauts study the geography, pollution, and weather patterns on Earth. They take many photographs to record their observations. Also, astronauts conduct

experiments on the shuttle to learn how space conditions, such as microgravity, affect humans, animals, plants, and insects. <u>Space shuttle astronauts exercise half an hour a day to stay healthy.</u>

(這個段落中劃底線的兩句談太空梭如何發射和載幾名太空人，以及他們每天運動時數，很明顯和這段的主題—太空人的工作無關，刪掉這兩句才能使段落有統一性。)

B. 連貫性 (**Coherence and Cohesion**)

(1) **Coherence** 是意義的連貫性，就是段落中要點或細節的安排要有一定的邏輯順序；句子和句子之間的邏輯關係要清楚。(例如：先有籠統 (general) 的敘述後有具體明確 (specific) 的細節、先提出問題後提解決方法、先提因後談果或先提果後談因、按時間的先後敘述或空間的遠近描述、從較不重要的要點到最重要的要點)。

(2) **Cohesion** 是文字語氣的連貫性，就是段落中運用適當的 words and phrases 使語氣流暢，句子之間環環相扣，包括：重複的關鍵字詞、代名詞、指示形容詞、以及承轉語 (transitions)。

a. Emotional symptoms can be disabling and unbearably painful, and can lead to feelings of fear, loneliness, and worthlessness. **These** symptoms can affect our ability to function and cope with activities of daily life. (這兩句以指示形容詞 **These** 達成連貫)
b. The shuttle does not use its engines for a landing. **It** glides through the atmosphere. (這兩句以代名詞 **It** 達成連貫)
c. Nowadays health specialists promote the idea of **wellness** for everybody. **Wellness** means achieving best possible health <u>within the limits of your body</u>. One person may need fewer calories than another. Some people might prefer a lot of easier <u>exercise</u> to more challenging <u>exercise</u>. While one person enjoys playing seventy-two holes of <u>golf</u> a week, another would rather play three sweaty, competitive games of <u>tennis</u>. (這個段落的連貫性是：第二句重複關鍵字 **wellness**，承接上一句。第二、三、四、五句的邏輯關係是第二句是一個 general statement，三、四句提出較明確的說明，而第五句又更明確地提出 golf 和 tennis 來解釋第四句提到的 exercise。)

 寫作練習

A. 由選項中先找出一個與主題無關的句子，再<u>重組</u>成連貫的段落。

(1) Every year tens of thousands of people come to admire Chatsworth House—the family home of the Dukes of Devonshire. The building of Chatsworth started in 1552 when Bess of Hardwick persuaded her husband, Sir William Cavendish to buy land in Derbyshire. _____

   (A) In the recently released film of *Pride and Prejudice*, it was used as the setting for Pemberley, the residence of Mr. Darcy.

   (B) After he died, his wife completed the building work, and left it to their son, William, who was made 1st Earl of Devonshire in 1618.

   (C) But he did not lived to see its completion.

   (D) The new Chatsworth was completed in 1707.

   (E) In 1685, the house began to be rebuilt by the 4th Earl, who was also 1st Duke.

(2) Depression is one of the most common problems people experience today. In the past, this emotional illness was thought to be nothing more than "the blues". _____

   (A) It not only provides a distraction from your worries but helps you get rid of built-up stress and frustration.

   (B) But there are some ways you can deal with depression on a daily basis.

   (C) Today people know that this illness is very real, and can be overcome.

   (D) For example, exercise is a helpful way to treat depression.

   (E) If you think you may be clinically depressed, the first step to take is to see a doctor.

   (F) Each year over 17 million American adults experience a period of clinical depression.

B. 將段落前的承轉語，填入適當空格，使成為連貫性的段落。

(1) | too; but; however; for example; so |

   The mind and body work together to produce stress, which is a bodily response to a stimulus, a response that disturbs the body's normal physiological balance. 1._____, stress is not always bad. 2._____, a stress reaction can sometimes save a person's life by releasing hormones that enable a person to react quickly and with greater energy in a dangerous situation. In everyday situations,

3._____, stress can provide that extra push needed to do something difficult.

4._____ too much stress often injures both the mind and the body and leads to a crisis or relapse. That's why it's so important to find ways to keep stress at a manageable level. There are several good suggestions in *Learn to Lighten Up and Live Longer*, the best seller of the month. 5._____, grab a copy and start learning how you can reduce stress in your life. (95 學測考題)

(2) | **on the other hand; as a result; however; on the contrary; to begin with; finally**

Fans of professional baseball and football argue continually over which is America's favorite sport. Though the figures on attendance for each vary with every new season, certain arguments remain the same. 1._____, football is a quicker, more physical sport, and football fans enjoy the emotional involvement they feel while watching. Baseball, 2._____, seems more mental, like chess, and attracts those fans that prefer a quieter, more complicated game. 3._____, professional football teams usually play no more than fourteen games a year. Baseball teams, 4._____, play almost every day for six months. 5._____, football fans seem to love the half-time activities, the marching bands, and the pretty cheerleaders. 6._____, baseball fans are more content to concentrate on the game's finer details and spend the breaks between innings filling out their own private scorecards. (95 學測考題)

Bow-bow Economics

As an increasing number of people begin to own pets, many companies around the world have been established to provide complete pet care. Actually, pet care companies are ___1___ so rapidly that most countries view them ___2___ an important economic stimulant.

In the US itself, there are about 60 million dog owners. Dogs are, ___3___, man's best friend, and it is natural that owners want the best for them. In order to cater to these people, a number of elite pet care companies have been established, such as *Hounds Tooth Bakery* and *Three Dog Bakery*. These companies are one-stop shops that ___4___ high-quality food, grooming facilities and other accessories for pets.

Regular pet shops merely sell basic supplies for pets, like toys and food. ___5___, some cafés are designed to provide dogs with the complete ___6___ experience. For example, *Munchies Pet Café* not only sells pet supplies and accessories but also provides an air-conditioned environment, plush seating, and ample running space for the dogs to eat and play. Moreover, it even ___7___ dog weddings and birthday parties.

Pet care is taken to yet another level by *Three Dog Bakery*, which has set up ___8___ is called *The Gracie Foundation*. This original foundation functions like a Canine Red Cross. It ___9___ the urgent needs of dogs in distress and provides them with food, medical attention, and funds.

Pet care is a growing business in countries as different as China, France, and America. As a result, many new companies have been set up to meet the ___10___ of pet owners. These companies are unique in that they target the pets as their customers and aim to pamper them as royalty.

_____ 1. (A) diminishing   (B) vanishing   (C) expanding   (D) extending

_____ 2. (A) of   (B) to   (C) as   (D) for

_____ 3. (A) therefore   (B) however   (C) above all   (D) after all

_____ 4. (A) provide   (B) reduce   (C) equip   (D) operate

_____ 5. (A) Moreover   (B) Consequently   (C) In fact   (D) In contrast

_____ 6. (A) shopping   (B) dining   (C) cooking   (D) walking

_____ 7. (A) rejects   (B) establishes   (C) organizes   (D) attends

_____ 8. (A) which   (B) what   (C) such   (D) so

_____ 9. (A) creates   (B) treats   (C) responds to   (D) corresponds to

_____ 10. (A) beliefs   (B) goals   (C) demands   (D) commands

UNIT 23

NOTE

 原來如此

1. **C** 由前一句 an increasing number of people 和 many companies 得知這類的公司擴充 (expanding) 迅速。(A) 減少 (B) 消失 (D) 延伸

2. **C** view...as(視為，認為) 和 regard...as 用法相同。

3. **D** after all (畢竟) 在表達原因或理由時使用。(C) 特別，尤其

4. **A** 本句後半的 for 是線索，provide...for (提供…給…)。

5. **D** 用 In contrast 來表達之後提到 bakeries、cafés 來和之前的 shops 對照說明。(A) 而且、再者 (B) 結果

6. **B** 下一句中的 eat 是重要線索，cafes 很特別的是提供用餐 (dining) 經驗。

7. **C** 籌畫 (organize) weddings, parties。(A) 拒絕 (B) 設立 (D) 參加

8. **B** what is called (所謂的) = what they call

9. **C** 對他人的需求做出回應 (respond to one's need)。(A) 創造 (B) 對待 (D) 與…一致，等於

10. **C** 由前文得知這類公司設立的目的是符合飼主的要求 (meet the demand)

 寫作練習

段落寫作練習單元 **1**

A. 以下有四個作文題目，每個題目之後有五至六個問題作為你構思的提示，參照這些提示寫出 100 字左右的段落短文。

(1) **My Favorite Snack/Drink/Dessert**

a. What is it?

b. Is it easy to make or get?

c. How can you prepare or make it?

d. How does it taste?

e. Why do you like it?

f. How do you feel after you enjoy it?

(2) **A Person I Admire Most**

a. Who is the person?

b. When/How did you know this person?

c. What does/did this person do?

d. How much do you understand this person?

e. What are the reasons you admire this person?

(3) **When I Get Angry**

    a. Do you often get angry?

    b. In what condition(s) do you get angry?

    c. What do you do when you get angry? Why?

    d. Is it the proper way to react like that?

    e. Is getting angry a bad thing or something constructive to you? Why?

(4) **A Problem/Problems I Have**

    a. As a teenager, what problems do you have, low self-esteem, low motivation, poor communication skills, or poor interpersonal relationships?

    b. How do they affect your life?

    c. Why do they trouble you a lot?

    d. Have you ever tried to cope with these problems?

    e. From whom can you seek help?

B. 下列有三組連環圖畫，根據圖畫內容將所發生的事件寫出合理的敘述 (120–150 字)。

(1)

(2)

(3)

 參考範例

B. (3) One day, when Lara was playing in a nearby park, two kidnappers grabbed her from the bicycle and put her in a car. Lara's dog saw the whole thing and wanted to save its little owner.

Soon the two kidnappers drove her to a deserted factory. The kidnappers bound Lara's hands and feet with rope; what's worse, she couldn't yell for help because her mouth was covered by a handkerchief. Then they called her father and told him they wanted a million dollars or he would never see Lara again. Later, the kidnappers went out and left Lara alone.

A few minutes later, something large and fast broke through the window. It was Lara's dog—it had followed her to the factory! Using its teeth, the dog untied Lara and they both escaped from the kidnappers and went home safe and sound. Thereafter, Lara and her dog became inseparable. She even called it Hero.

NOTE

A Day without Laughter is a Day Wasted

In Mumbai, India, at six thirty every morning, a group of more than one hundred people meet at a neighborhood park for exercise. These people are both men and women, and are ___1___ all different ages and levels of fitness. Being in India, you might expect that this is a yoga group, or perhaps they go jogging together or practice aerobics. ___2___, this is a laughter club.

Laughter clubs began in 1995 and since then have ___3___ to other parts of India and more than 40 countries around the world. A qualified laughter teacher ___4___ the session which normally begins with some deep breathing and stretching exercises. Then the participants stand around ___5___ a circle and try different types of laughing, like dancing laughing, hearty laughing and giggling. Each session ___6___ for between 20 and 30 minutes.

You might think that you need to watch a funny movie or hear a joke to laugh, but this isn't true. Just listening to someone else laugh can make you laugh, and the more you laugh, ___7___ you feel. When you are laughing, you cannot feel pain, fear, anger or boredom. Some people believe that an important step to world peace would be for every person in the world to laugh every day.

One of the best things about laughing is that it's without ___8___. Participants can be of any age, and they do not need any special clothing or equipment. People of both sexes and from different ___9___ of life can participate, including doctors, managers, workers, and peddlers. Even people from other countries who speak different languages can ___10___, because laughter is a language that all humans understand. ___11___, participants don't have to be rich. Laughter is free!

Many companies have now started laughter clubs for their employees because it ___12___ stress and increases productivity. The members of laughter clubs say that laughing makes them feel refreshed, relaxed and revitalized. With results like these, we could all do with a laugh!

_____ 1. (A) on   (B) at   (C) of   (D) under

_____ 2. (A) In addition   (B) In contrast   (C) In fact   (D) Accordingly

_____ 3. (A) spread   (B) scattered   (C) transmitted   (D) infected

_____ 4. (A) records   (B) leads   (C) occupies   (D) entertains

_____ 5. (A) in   (B) on   (C) of   (D) above

_____ 6. (A) longs   (B) lasts   (C) continues   (D) stands

_____ 7. (A) the more likely   (B) the more happily   (C) the more   (D) the happier

_____ 8. (A) limitation   (B) disadvantages   (C) response   (D) damage

_____ 9. (A) forms   (B) cycles   (C) walks   (D) styles

_____ 10. (A) join in   (B) take over   (C) give in   (D) head for

_____ 11. (A) That is to say   (B) In other words   (C) Best of all   (D) On the other hand

_____ 12. (A) raises   (B) dismisses   (C) regains   (D) reduces

NOTE

 原來如此

1. **C** people of different ages (不同年齡的人)。
2. **C** 空格前提出猜測，空格後點出事實，所以此處要選擇 in fact(事實上)。
3. **A** (A) 消息或想法的傳播 (B) 散播，散置 (C) 傳送 (D) 感染
4. **B** 老師帶領 (leads) 這集會 (session)。
5. **A** in a circle (圍成圓圈)。
6. **B** 由空格之後 for...minutes 得知要選 last (持續)。(A) long for... (期望) (D) stand for (代表)
7. **D** 此為句型 the more/-er..., the more/-er。由空格之後 feel 判斷此格需要一個形容詞而非副詞，所以選 the happier (越快樂)。
8. **A** 由此段文意 (任何人都可參加) 可以知道這個主題句表達的是「笑是沒有限制的」。
9. **C** 由 including 之後所列的各行業可得知此處用 different walks of life (不同行業)。
10. **A** join in (參加)。(B) 接管 (C) 屈服 (D) 前往
11. **C** 段落最後一句提出另一個優點，用 best of all (最好的是) 引出句子。
12. **D** reduce 和 increase 是反義字，reduce stress (減少緊張)。

 寫作練習

段落寫作練習單元 **2**

A. 以下是一則現代寓言，仔細閱讀後把你的感想寫成一個段落短文。(包括寓言之寓意，以及寓言給你的啟示)

　　A large spider in an old house built a beautiful web in which to catch flies. Every time a fly landed on the web and was entangled in it, the spider devoured him so that when another fly came along he would think the web was a safe and quiet place in which to rest. One day a fairly intelligent fly buzzed around above the web so long that the spider appeared and said, "Come on down." But the fly was too clever for him and said, "I never settle where I don't see other flies and I don't see any other flies in your house." So he flew away until he came to a place where there were a great many other flies. He was about to settle down among them when a bee buzzed up and said, "Hold it, stupid, that's flypaper. All those flies are trapped." "Don't be silly," said the fly, "they're dancing." So he settled down and became stuck to the flypaper with all the other flies.

by James Thurber

UNIT 24

B. 將圖畫中發生的事件合理地敘述出來。

C. 使用過去時態把這個夢境敘述完成

    After a tiring day, I went to bed earlier than usual. However, shortly after I closed my eyes, I heard a strange sound of music. _____

_____

_____

_____

_____

_____

When I opened my eyes, I found my Mom tried to wake me up by shaking my body. What an unusual dream!!

D. 根據以下的提示，寫成一段 150 字的短文。
  (1) **"My Favorite Tourist Spot in Taiwan"**
    Topic Sentence: what your favorite tourist spot is and where it is
    Supporting Details: the reasons why it attracts you

Concluding Sentence: a suggestion to the reader

(2) **"How I Deal With Stress"**
  Topic Sentence: your special or practical ways to deal with stress
  Supporting Sentences: what the ways are, how they help reduce stress, and how
          you feel after you do the activities
  Concluding Sentence: restate the ways you cope with stress before it beats you

 參考範例

A. This fable talks about the fact that a clever person sometimes can be ruined by his or her own cleverness. In the story, the clever fly buzzed around, looking for a safe spot. The fly was clever enough to avoid falling into the spider's trap. Later on, however, when it found a place where many flies were "dancing," it decided to rest there in spite of the bee's warning. The self-conceited fly met its doom just because it only believed in its own judgment. Unfortunately, it would never have a chance to learn from its fatal experience, and this does happen in our life, too.

International Eating

In any large city in the United States or Canada , you can find many international restaurants. __1__ there are many immigrants in large cities who open restaurants and because Americans like ethnic food. There is a wide __2__ of cooking styles and foods __3__ by these restaurants. In San Francisco, __4__ , you can find French, Italian, Chinese, Mexican, Japanese, and Vietnamese restaurants.

International restaurants offer a variety of options. First, some of them are __5__ , such as French and Italian. Many families celebrate a special event __6__ in an elegant French or Italian restaurant, where __7__ many courses in a meal. __8__ , some international food is cheap. Many Mexican and Chinese restaurants __9__ large meals that are not very expensive. Finally, some kinds of ethnic foods are __10__ . For example, Japanese restaurants serve fresh fish and vegetables cooked with little fat.

So, if you live in a city in North America, you can eat in an Iranian restaurant __11__ and in a Mexican restaurant the next. You can enjoy __12__ dishes and learn about food from all over the world.

_____ 1. (A) Where   (B) Since   (C) This is why   (D) This is because

_____ 2. (A) collection   (B) range   (C) horizon   (D) species

_____ 3. (A) represented   (B) replaced   (C) preserved   (D) prevented

_____ 4. (A) therefore   (B) however   (C) for example   (D) as a result

_____ 5. (A) ordinary   (B) fancy   (C) expansive   (D) spacious

_____ 6. (A) to eat   (B) to serve   (C) by serving   (D) by eating

_____ 7. (A) there maybe   (B) there may be   (C) they may be   (D) it may be

_____ 8. (A) In addition to   (B) In other words   (C) Besides   (D) Conversely

_____ 9. (A) reserve   (B) serve   (C) consume   (D) demand

_____ 10. (A) strange   (B) processed   (C) calorific   (D) healthful

_____ 11. (A) one night   (B) at night   (C) at noon   (D) another noon

_____ 12. (A) home-made   (B) usual   (C) exotic   (D) indigestible

原來如此

1. **D** 由一二句之間的邏輯得知第一句表結果、第二句表原因,因此選 (D)。

2. **B** a wide range of 指「範圍很廣的,各種各類的」。
   (A) 收集 (C) 地平線 (D) 種類

3. **A** represent 指「代表」;represented by... 是過去分詞片語修飾 foods。
   (B) 代替 (C) 保存 (D) 防止

4. **C** 以 San Francisco 為例說明 there are many international restaurants in any large city,因此選 for example。(A) 因此 (B) 然而 (D) 結果

5. **B** fancy 指「高級的」,由下一句 celebrate a special event 及 elegant 可以得知不是「普通的」。(A) 普通的 (C) 寬闊的 (D) 寬敞的

6. **D** by + V-ing 指「藉著…方式」,以在餐廳吃飯的方式慶祝,因此用 by eating。
   (A) to eat 為不定詞表目的

7. **B** there may be 指「或許有」,may 是助動詞之後加原形動詞 be。

8. **C** 由文意得知本句提出第二個理由,因此用表達增加的連貫詞 besides 或 in addition (此外)。(A) 除…之外 (B) 換句話說 (D) 相反地

9. **B** serve large meals 供應盛餐。(A) 預定,保留 (C) 消耗,消費 (D) 要求

10. **D** 由下一句的 fresh fish and vegetables cooked with little fat 得知此題選 healthful (有益健康的)。(A) 奇怪的 (B) 加工處理的 (C) 產生熱量的

11. **A** one night...the next (night) 表示某一個晚上和第二天晚上。

12. **C** 由 Mexican restaurant 和 Iranian restaurant 得知此題選 exotic (有異國風味的)。(A) 自製的 (D) 不易消化的

寫作要點

文章 (Essay) 的寫作要領

A. 文章的結構和寫法:

一般來說,Essay 指的是包含有三段以上至八段的文章。但是高中生的作文,不論是學科測驗或是指定考科的英文作文,都規定在 120 字左右。因此你可以選擇把內容在一段之中表達完整,也可以分成兩段、三段或四段表達。

文章有三個主要的部分:引言 (Introduction)、主體 (Body) 和結論 (Conclusion)。

(1) 引言 (Introduction):

引言的功能是吸引讀者和點出文章的主旨。高中生的作文此部份只需要兩三句即可。引言通常包含兩個主要的部分①主題導引 (lead-in) 在頭一兩句,用來吸引讀

者，導入正題。通常用一些背景資料 (例如：提出問題、有趣的事實或數據、或引用名人的話)。②主旨陳述 (**thesis statement**) 通常是這段的最後一句，它預告文章內容，也就是文章的主旨。尤其在說明文及議論文中，這個句子非常重要。

a. 這段引言一開始就用了問句和答句來引起注意：

Who is more stressed out — Asian teenagers or American teenagers? Surprisingly, American teens win the contest....

b. 這段引言用了兩個問句作為主題導引，而主旨陳述則是劃底線的部分。

Are you someone who practically lives in front of the computer—a mouse potato? Or are you nervous about new technology—a technophobe? In either case, if you want to master the English language, <u>you will need to be familiar with those new computer words that seem to be popping up everywhere.</u>

(2) 主體 (**Body**)：

主體部份可以視需要分成幾個段落，這些段落要能支持及闡明主旨 (**thesis**)。每一段要有主題句和支持細節，且是完整的段落結構。關於段落寫作，請參考 Unit 19 寫作要點。而段與段之間要注意語氣連貫，可以使用代名詞、重述前段的字或要點、或者用承轉語詞 (transitional expressions)。

(3) 結論 (**Conclusion**)：

結論必須簡潔有力，可以是用不同的文字重述主旨陳述 (thesis statement) 或提出問題、建議、解決之道。例如：

a. So, grab a copy and start learning how you can reduce stress in your life.

b. An old proverb says, "Truth is stranger than fiction." Do you think that's true?

B. 大綱 (outline)

一般同學常常是看到題目後，提筆就寫，邊想邊寫，常導致作文沒有條理，結構鬆散或無法節制而離題太遠。因此要寫出層次分明、結構嚴謹的文章，最好拿筆記下想到的要點，去蕪存菁之後，把要點有組織地排列整理成大綱，再依此寫成文章。

大綱範例：

Introduction: lead-in —"Laugh and the whole world laughs with you. Weep and you weep alone."

thesis statement —A good laugh a day keeps the doctor away.

Body: Topic sentence —Laughter keeps us healthy.

Point 1 —Laughter is the best preventive medicine for heart disease.

Point 2 —Laughter helps strengthen our immune system.

Point 3 —Laughter reduces stress and lowers our blood pressure.

Conclusion: Why not let laughter be part of a daily health routine—just like getting exercise and eating healthy food?

C. 四種常用的文體：

記敘文 (narration)、描寫文 (description)、說明文 (exposition)、議論文 (argumentation)，分別在 Unit 26 至 Unit 29 四個單元詳細介紹寫作要點。

寫作練習

A. 根據 p. 117 的大綱範例以 "Laughter is the Best Medicine" 為題寫成一篇包括三段，150 字左右的作文。

B. 請根據以下的大綱，以 "My Favorite Season" 為題寫成一篇包括三段，120 ～ 150 字左右的作文。

Introduction: my favorite season and the reason

Body: point 1—what you often see in this season

point 2—how you feel in this season

point 3 —something special you like to do in this season

Conclusion: explain the reason in different words

參考範例

A.　　Perhaps most of us are familiar with the saying "Laugh and the whole world laughs with you. Weep and you weep alone." However, did you know that research has shown that laughter has both preventive and healing values? Maybe a good laugh a day can really keep the doctor away.

　　Laughter helps improve our health in several ways. If we are at high risk of having heart disease, laughter could be the best preventive medicine. That's because laughter improves the blood circulation and oxygen supply to the heart muscles. Laughter also encourages the production of white blood cells and increases our resistance to infection. Thus, our immune system is strengthened. The immune system is the master key for maintaining good health. Besides, laughter is found to reduce stress and lower blood pressure. Stress is one of the major causes for blood pressure. Laughter definitely helps you control blood pressure by reducing the release of stress hormones and bringing relaxation.

　　Laughter really is the best medicine. Why not let laughter be part of a daily health routine—just like exercise and a healthy diet?

NOTE

A Pacific Paradise Tour

文意選填：由下列單字中選最適當者填入空格中 (請注意大小寫)

at	after	with	also	so	next	last
finally	all	went	watching	forget	has	tour

A Pacific Paradise Tour took us to California, on the west coast of the United States, and to Hawaii in the Pacific Ocean. (1) _____ beautiful countryside, exciting cities and fantastic beaches, this trip had everything.

The first place we stopped (2) _____ was San Francisco. This city is famous for its cable cars and people certainly needs them because San Francisco is extremely hilly and has some very steep roads! By the sea, (3) _____ to the fishing boats, there are many fish restaurants. Here we enjoyed watching the street actors and musicians as we ate delicious fresh fish. One thing we would never (4) _____ is the Golden Gate Bridge, which is very big and beautiful.

The next city on the (5) _____ was Los Angeles. This city is very exciting and (6) _____ some very famous attractions. The nearby beaches are long and sandy. We visited the beach where *Baywatch* had been filmed. We (7) _____ went to Disneyland where we shook hands with Mickey Mouse. (8) _____ that, we were taken to Hollywood to see the houses of the actors and actresses who have starred in a lot of films and made a lot of money!

The (9) _____ place we visited in California was San Diego, a city with sunshine, sand, sea and all kinds of water sports. We went to the San Diego Zoo, which is one of the world's largest zoos.

(10) _____, we went to Hawaii. It's indeed a paradise! We sat on golden beaches with green palm trees and watched amazing red sunsets. We also saw colorful fish at Sea Life Park and (11) _____ snorkeling in Hanauma Bay. In the evenings we enjoyed the lively clubs, bars and ice-cream parlors. Best of (12)

_____, we ate fantastic Hawaiian food while (13) _____ Hawaiian people performing traditional Polynesian dances.

This holiday was fantastic. (14) _____ when you have time, get on the first plane to the west coast of the United States and have a good time!

NOTE

原來如此

1.	**With**	用 with 片語表達 this trip had everything 的原因。
2.	**at**	stop at 停留於
3.	**next**	next to 在…隔壁
4.	**forget**	用 we'll never forget 來強調對這個景點印象深刻
5.	**tour**	on the tour 在旅遊中
6.	**has**	has 的主詞是 the city。
7.	**also**	also (也) 是副詞，用來從上一個景點承接到下一個景點。
8.	**After**	after that (在那之後) 引出下一個景點。
9.	**last**	本段要敘述的是在 California 遊覽的最後一個地點。
10.	**Finally**	以下是旅遊最後一站，因此選 finally。
11.	**went**	go snorkeling 去浮潛
12.	**all**	best of all 是片語，用來表達與前面幾項相較之下，接下來要提的是最好的。
13.	**watching**	while watching 是由 while we were watching 變化而來的分詞結構。
14.	**So**	so (所以) 是連接詞。

寫作要點

記敘文及短文解析

A. 記敘文 **Narration**

　　記敘文敘述經驗或事件發生的經過。例如傳記、遊記、故事都屬於記敘文。要點的安排通常按照時間順序，可以採順序法，或採倒序法追述過去。本篇克漏字短文是一篇遊記，依照「時間順序」記載遊覽地點及特色。

B. Cloze 短文解析

1. 引言 (**Introduction**)：

　　只有兩句，很清楚明確地說出遊覽的兩大部分 (California and Hawaii) 而且玩得盡興 (this trip had everything)，這就是本篇作文的 central idea。

2. 主體 (**Body**)：

　　按時間順序，重點式地提出三個城市與夏威夷，分成四段，運用承轉語 the first、next、last 和 finally 使段落之間文氣流暢。每段依次敘述不同的景點及特色。注意段落中的時態 (tense) 現在式與過去式交錯。用現在式的句子很明顯表達的是事實，而非旅遊經歷。旅遊經歷發生在過去就用過去式。

(1) 以第三段為例，第二句是主題句，第三句以後列舉三個 attractions (beach, Disneyland, Hollywood)，用承轉語 also 和 after that 巧妙地使句子連貫。

(2) 以第五段為例，要點的安排並非按照時間順序，而是以精彩程度或者重要性安排，因此作者把最喜歡的項目放在最後，用片語 best of all 引出。

3. 結語 (**Conclusion**)：

只有兩句，但是就用了寫結語的兩種方法：

(1)「重述主題」：

作者用了與引言 the holiday had everything 相呼應的 the holiday was fantastic。

(2)「向讀者提出呼籲」：

作者呼籲讀者立刻採取行動 get on the first plane to the west coast of the United States。

※本篇短文可以學到：

(1) 前言和結語都只有兩句，清楚明白，結語更是簡單巧妙，和主題句相呼應，很適合高中程度的同學學習。

(2) 按時間或空間順序排列要點。

(3) 因為列舉景點，因而巧妙地運用了大量的承轉語。

Extra (1) 表示「列舉」的承轉語

first, firstly, first of all, in the first place, second, secondly, third, finally, best of all, most important of all, last of all, last but not least

(2) 表示「時間」及「空間」的承轉語

at the same time, once, since then, ever since, at last, later, after that, next, earlier, at first, then, the next day, from then on, in the beginning, beside, across, from...to, up, down, near, far

---

寫作練習

敘述經歷時，就像說故事，一開始就要交代場景、時間、地點、人物、事件及結局。請參考以下的範例作文之後，以 A(n) ＿＿＿ Experience 為題，寫一篇 120 字至 150 字左右的作文。

A Frightening Experience

It was a winter flight from Taipei to New York. As usual, it was long and boring. Luckily, the airline I chose had personal television installed on every seat. I remember I just watched a movie and felt tired, so I decided to take a nap. All of a sudden, the aircraft shook dramatically. At first I thought it was simply turbulence, and it would last a few seconds and end soon, just as other cases of turbulence I had experienced before. However, this time it didn't end, at least not in seconds. My chocolate cake on the table, which I saved from the meal for snack, fell on the floor, and I didn't have time to feel sorry because the plane immediately dropped a bit. During the few seconds of dropping, it felt like the plane was going to crash—who knew it wouldn't? This falling scared everybody, including me; my hands were sweaty. Some girls started screaming. I thought that was it—I was going to die in Alaska! I tried to think if there was anything I should think up before death, and realized that there was not much coming up to my mind. Thank God. Nothing worse happened after that. After another six hours we landed in New York.

B. 請以下列題目練習作文

(1) "A Dream I Had Last Night"

(2) "A Dream That Came True"

(3) "My Last Winter/Summer Vacation"

(4) "My First Day in Senior High School"

(5) "The Best Day in My Life"

(6) "An Experience of Winning/Losing a Game"

NOTE

My Goals in Life

Like everyone else, I have many goals in life. Two of the most important are getting a solid education and ___1___ a healthy planet for those who come after me.

At first, I want an education that will not only prepare me to get a well-paying and worthwhile job but ___2___ will also help me live a satisfying life. To prepare myself to get a good job, I am majoring in X-ray technology. Careers in radiology pays quite well. I would be able to ___3___ myself and my family comfortably; and some day, perhaps, I would be able to buy a house in a safe neighborhood with good schools. But I also want to get ___4___ a liberal education. For example, I want to take courses in literature and the arts to ___5___ my leisure time. I want to take courses in psychology and sociology to understand myself and my fellow citizens. I also want to take courses in ___6___ to see where we humans have come from and where we are headed.

Protecting the environment is also important to me. ___7___ everyone else, I have a duty to leave our Earth in at least so good a condition as I found it. I believe we should all be like those Native Americans whose religion required them ___8___ how their actions would affect the seventh generation of those who followed. One small contribution I can make is to limit the size of my family so as not to ___9___ the exploding population growth that threatens the environment and the quality of life for everyone. I can also ___10___ those political candidates who can look further into the future than the next election.

No one wants to live in ___11___, but it is not necessary for us to be rich to be happy, ___12___ our education has prepared us to lead a full life. At the same time, we cannot be happy if we are leaving to our grandchildren an unhealthy planet.

126

_____ 1. (A) to leave   (B) leaving   (C) to give   (D) giving

_____ 2. (A) that   (B) what   (C) it   (D) this

_____ 3. (A) offend   (B) defend   (C) support   (D) attain

_____ 4. (A) it is called   (B) to be called   (C) which is called   (D) what is called

_____ 5. (A) enrich   (B) take   (C) enlarge   (D) full

_____ 6. (A) geography   (B) physics   (C) history   (D) chemistry

_____ 7. (A) Unlike   (B) Like   (C) Dislike   (D) Alike

_____ 8. (A) thinking of   (B) thinking over   (C) to regard   (D) to consider

_____ 9. (A) contribute to   (B) help to   (C) tend to   (D) yield to

_____ 10. (A) care for   (B) go in for   (C) reach for   (D) vote for

_____ 11. (A) poverty   (B) comfort   (C) circumstances   (D) frustration

_____ 12. (A) as if   (B) especially if   (C) however   (D) accordingly

UNIT 27

NOTE

原來如此

1. **B** leaving 與 getting 是前後對稱的結構；leave...for 把…留給。

2. **A** that 子句和上一行的 that 子句同樣是關係子句修飾 education。

3. **C** support myself and my family 養活自己和家人。
   (A) 冒犯，得罪 (B) 防衛，防守 (D) 達成，達到

4. **D** what is called (所謂的) 是一個插入的關係子句。

5. **A** enrich 使豐富。(C) 擴大 (D) full (Adj.) 滿的

6. **C** 由之後的文意得知此題選歷史學科。(A) 地理 (B) 物理 (D) 化學

7. **B** like (*prep.*) (A) 不像 (C) 不喜歡 (D) 相同地

8. **D** require (要求) someone to do something，consider 在此字義是考慮。
   (A) 想起來 (B) 仔細考慮 (C) 認為

9. **A** contribute to + N. 有助於，成為…的原因。(B) help to + V. (C) tend to + V. 傾向於 (D) yield to + N. 向…屈服

10. **D** 由之後的 candidates (候選人) 得知此題選 vote for (投票給)。
    (A) 照顧，喜歡 (B) 喜歡 (C) 伸手去拿

11. **A** 由之後的 rich 得知此題選 poverty (貧窮)。(B) 舒適 (C) 情況 (D) 挫折

12. **B** 此句是集合句，此處仍需要一個從屬連接詞 (可以由三個子句需要兩個連接詞接連成一句的觀念來分辨)，因此選 especially if。as if (好像) 也是從屬連接詞，但語意不合。(C) however (然而) 和 (D) accordingly (所以) 都是承轉語 (transitions)，詞性是副詞。

寫作練習

說明文及短文解析

A. 說明文 **Exposition**

(1) 說明文通常解釋說明事情、觀念和方法。

(2) 常見的題目如 "My Hobby"、"My Philosophy of Life"、"Good Sportsmanship"、"How to Read" 之類的題目，通常以列舉事實、說明理由、下定義的方式擴展主題。要點常以重要順序安排。本篇作者說明其人生目標，就是說明文。

(3) 在四種文體中，說明文是非常需要在引言 (Introduction) 部分有一個主旨陳述 (thesis statement) 的句子，它是表達整篇作文主旨 (main idea) 的句子，功能就像是作者的計畫，計畫作文要寫什麼，也讓讀者由第一段即可知道一篇文章的 central idea。

B. Cloze 短文解析

1. 引言 (**Introduction**)：

只有兩句，第二句 Two of the most important are getting a solid education and leaving a healthy planet for those who come after me. 就是「主旨陳述」。

2. 主體 (**Body**)：

則依此分成兩段分別說明。第二段的第一句是主題句，以大綱列出顯示其段落層次如下：

> Get a well-paying and worthwhile job
>   (1) Support myself and my family
>   (2) Buy a house
> Live a satisfying life
>   (1) Courses in literature and the arts
>   (2) Courses in psychology and sociology
>   (3) Courses in history

第三段第一句是主題句。以下擴展主題句的部分，

作者先以 I believe we should all be like those Native Americans... 提出說明他注重環保的理由。之後兩句提出他的做法 One small contribution I can make is... 和下一句的 I can also vote for...。

3. 結語 (**Conclusion**)：

作者對整篇內容簡略地摘要重述 ...our education has prepared us to lead a full life... 及 we cannot be happy if we are leaving to our grandchildren....。人稱從 I 轉成 we，有些呼籲的功能，希望讀者能與其觀念一致。

※本篇短文可以學到：

(1) 簡短明確的前言。

(2) 第二段和第三段第一句都是很好的主題句，值得仿效。

(3) 第二段和第三段支持主題句細節安排層次分明，仔細看上面列出的大綱即可知。兩段說明了什麼目標、原因、以及現在做了什麼、將來又能做什麼。

(4) 結語兩句各自把兩項目標簡略做了摘要，是很值得學習的。

Extra

(1) 表示「因果」的承轉語

because, for the reason, therefore, as a result, consequently, so, so that, thus, hence, accordingly, in short, otherwise, then

(2) 強調「事實」的承轉語

in fact, as a matter of fact, no doubt, doubtless, undoubtedly, without a doubt

寫作練習

A. 學校的課業壓力大嗎？與同學相處困難嗎？你氣餒、沮喪、心情不好的時候，有什麼排遣的方法呢？請參考以下的範例之後，以 "How I Encourage Myself When I Fail" 或者 "When I Am Feeling Down" 為題寫一篇 120 到 150 字左右的作文。

When I Am in a Bad Mood

As a senior high school student, I am really under a lot of stress because of the numerous exams and the interaction with my classmates. The stress sometimes puts me in a bad mood, and I will try every possible way to get rid of it.

If I come back home from school with my bad mood, I will hurry into my room and get a short story with a happy ending to read. From those stories, I share the joys and sorrows of the characters and realize that ups and downs surely exist. What's more, happy endings always give me hope. Besides readings, sometimes after dinner I will offer to help do the washing. When I wash the dirty dishes, I not only clean them up but also clean away my bad mood. Thus bad grades or the cruel words my classmates have said to me are gone with the water. Before I start to review my lessons, I usually spend some time playing with my pet, a black cat. She is really like my younger sister. When we play hide-and-seek, she often does something stupid. Every time she hides herself under the blanket, she leaves her tail outside. When she gets caught, her puzzled look always makes me laugh and laugh, which releases me from my pent-up sadness and anger.

These are the ways I deal with my bad mood, and they do work. When I go back to school, I feel happier, and stronger to face the stress of my school life.

B. 請以下列題目練習作文
   (1) "How to Be a Good Friend"
   (2) "How to Ease Depression"
   (3) "A Lesson I Learned"
   (4) "My Career Plan"
   (5) "Something That Money Can't Buy"

A Bicycle Trip in Kuanshan

In the warm spring, when flowers are blooming, where can you go on the weekend? If you choose to soak in a hot spring or appreciate the cherry blossoms, __1__ are that you won't escape the crowds. How about coming to Kuanshan, Taitung, to enjoy a bicycle trip that __2__ exercise and sightseeing?

The town is ringed by a 12-kilometer bicycle trail. Much of the trail follows the Peinan River, the Hungshih Creek, and the Kuanshan Irrigation Channel. So all along the route you are __3__ by the sound of water and can enjoy waterside scenery.

As you advance along the route, the scenes change too. Eight kilometers along the trail, endless rice fields __4__ into the distance. With the murmur of the creek and with the mildness of the breeze, you may feel carefree and happy as if transported __5__ a Jean Millet painting. Besides the creek, you can see the bamboos __6__ in the wind. Some of their leaves carelessly flutter down onto the water and __7__ down the stream. When you keep going down, you'll have the delightful experience of winding your way through a garden __8__ with fallen yellow leaves. You can hear the rustle of dry leaves under your wheels and the song of birds in the trees.

Near the end of the trail you may __9__ upon a field full of flowering rape. Tens of thousands of golden flowers are tossing their heads, fluttering and dancing in the breeze. Stop your bicycle and take a photo amid the beautiful golden fields. The photo can __10__ the joy that the bicycle trip in Kuanshan brings you.

_____ 1. (A) sights   (B) reasons   (C) chances   (D) situations
_____ 2. (A) relates   (B) concludes   (C) confused   (D) combines
_____ 3. (A) accompanied   (B) disturbed   (C) interrupted   (D) shocked
_____ 4. (A) lengthen   (B) break   (C) stretch   (D) develop
_____ 5. (A) through   (B) into   (C) for   (D) at
_____ 6. (A) drifting   (B) swaying   (C) to drift   (D) to sway
_____ 7. (A) float   (B) flap   (C) twist   (D) grow
_____ 8. (A) is covered   (B) carpeted   (C) is lying   (D) spreading
_____ 9. (A) look   (B) fall   (C) call   (D) come
_____ 10. (A) impress   (B) imitate   (C) record   (D) remain

原來如此

1. **C** 如果去泡湯或賞櫻，躲不開人群是很可能的。chances are (that)... 有可能。
   (A) 景象，視界 (B) 理由 (D) 情況
2. **D** bicycle trip 可以讓你運動和看風景。combine 結合，合併。
   (A) 與…有關連 (B) 下結論 (C) 使困惑
3. **A** 一路上水聲陪伴，be accompanied by 由…陪伴。
   (B) 打擾 (C) 打擾，打斷談話 (D) 使震驚
4. **C** stretch 綿延，延伸；stretch into the distance 綿延至遠處。
   (A) 加長 (B) break into 闖入 (D) 發展
5. **B** be transported into a painting 被帶入畫中；as if transported into... 是 as if you were transported into... 的省略。
6. **B** sway 搖擺，swaying in the wind 隨風飄動，sway + ing 是因為之前的是感官動詞 see。
7. **A** float down the stream 順流而下。(B) 飄動 (C) 扭曲 (D) 生長
8. **B** 佈滿黃葉可以說 be covered/carpeted with fallen yellow leaves；(A) 要改為 which is covered，用關係子句修飾 garden 才正確；carpet 名詞用法是地毯，動詞用法則是指「像地毯一般覆蓋」。
9. **D** come upon 偶然間遇到
10. **C** 照片的功能是記錄，因此選 record。
    (A) 使有印象 (B) 模仿 (D) 留下，仍然是

寫作練習

描寫文及短文解析

A. 描寫文 **Description**
描寫文通常描述人物、景色或物品。寫作的要點如下：
(1) 取材要有特色。
(2) 文字要生動。
(3) 要點的安排可以按照空間順序，或是從籠統到細節有層次地描述。常見的主題有描述畫、照片、圖片、地點、人物或街景。

本篇作者寫作的目的是藉著描繪單車道沿途的景色，以景誘人，吸引讀者前往；因此是一篇描寫文。

B. Cloze 短文解析

在十二公里的行程當中，景色無數，作者經取捨之後只選了四個最特殊的題材，加強描寫，由車道的起點至終點依空間順序排列。

(1) 置身 rice field 被比喻為在 Millet 的畫中。

(2) "bamboos are swaying in the wind, leaves carelessly flutter down onto the water and float along the stream"，讀者彷彿看到竹葉水上流。

(3) "hear the rustle of dry leaves under your wheels"，讀者彷彿聽到車輪踩落葉的聲音。

(4) 描寫金黃色的油菜花時，作者模仿 William Wordsworth 的詩 Daffodils 中的詩句 "tens of thousands of golden flowers are tossing their heads, fluttering and dancing in the breeze" 讀者彷彿看到千萬朵油菜花，搔首弄姿在微風中飄舞。讀者看到的就是一幅動態的圖畫。

在最後一句，作者很巧妙地藉由拍照寫出愉快單車行的終點，這是很好的收尾，和第一段的呼籲 (come to enjoy a bicycle trip) 相呼應。

※本篇短文可以學到：

(1) 要點以「空間次序」流暢地安排。

(2) 選材要取捨，選擇較有特色或是好發揮的題材。

(3) 運用想像力和聯想力，將靜態的景緻做動態的描寫。

※描寫人物也是描寫文常見的主題，寫人物和寫景一樣要抓住其特色。

　　如果題目是 "My Mother/Father/Sister" 之類較廣範圍的，可以在審題時下工夫做選擇，在有點題功能的 Introduction 中把範圍限制在外觀、個性的特色，再加上與作者的互動關係會比較吸引讀者。如九十學年度學科能力測驗作文題目 "Something Interesting about a Classmate of Mine"，題材就已經限制在有趣的部分了；可以是外觀上、動作上或個性上的有趣，抓住有特色的兩項發揮，最好舉出一兩件他或她做的趣事來證明。描寫人、物、景都是要平日就能細心觀察，用心感受的，修辭方面也是要多模仿學習，例如形容詞的運用、比喻用法、擬人技巧等等。

Extra
(1) 表示「舉例」的承轉語
　　for example, for instance, such as, in other words, namely, that is, in particular
(2) 表示「增加」的承轉語
　　in addition, besides, another, furthermore, moreover, and then, further, likewise

寫作練習

A. 描寫一幅你喜歡的畫、雜誌上的圖片、旅遊照片或者小時候的照片。參考以下範例作文之後，先回答以下問題：

(1) 作者掌握這幅畫的哪個特色？

(2) 作者如何安排描述畫中所看到的景象？是否由畫中的焦點到兩旁，再到後方 reflection 的部分？畫帶給觀賞者什麼感受？

(3) 以 "A Description of a Painting/Picture/Photo" 為題寫一篇 120 至 150 字左右的作文。

> **A Description of a Painting**
>
> *A Bar at the Folies-Bergéres* is an interesting painting by Edward Manet, a French painter in the 19th century. The bartender, a young girl, stands behind the counter in the center of the painting with her hands laying on the edge of the counter. She seems lost in her thoughts. On both sides of the counter, there are bottles of wine; two roses in a vase and a bowl of fruit are on her left. What is behind her looks a little vague. On our left, it seems that there is an extended space where we find a table with two bottles of wine. But if we look at the right, we can see the girl's back and realize that the whole scene is simply a reflection of a mirror. However, in the reflection, we see a gentleman talking to the bartender, and we don't see him in the foreground. This leads the whole painting to the extreme ambiguity: What does the reflection exactly mean? Which is real, the scene in the mirror or outside the mirror? Can a mirror really "mirror" our lives? I think this is what makes this painting interesting since Manet throws questions for us to wonder but does not seem to provide a definite answer. It gives space for all the viewers to contemplate.

B. 請以下列題目練習作文：

(1) "A Peaceful Country Scene"

(2) "The Horrific Scene After the 921 Earthquake"

(3) "Something That You Hear and See on Your Trip"

(4) "A Person That I Want to Interview"

(5) "My Favorite Character in a Novel"

(6) "An Interesting Character in a Story"

Competition

文意選填：由下列單字中選最適當者填入空格中(請注意大小寫)

conclude	lie	improve	encourage	known	do	effort
drawbacks	support	industry	wages	beneficial	against	however

Much can be said (1) _____ the desire to come first. As Bernard Hunt, a British journalist said, "Winning is a drug. Once you have experienced it, you cannot (2) _____ without it." However, competition has long been the driving force behind improvements in areas such as world trade and sports performance.

The main disadvantage of competition is that it can (3) _____ dishonesty. This is illustrated by the large numbers of athletes who are disqualified from events every year for having taken drugs to (4) _____ their performance. Politicians have also been (5) _____ to be untruthful especially when they want to win an election so much that they will (6) _____ to get votes. In (7) _____, the competition to produce more goods at cheaper prices is so intense that it can lead companies to open factories in poor countries. There they can exploit employees by making them work long hours for low (8) _____.

On the other hand, competition in sport means that athletes have to make the greatest (9) _____ they can. This is an exciting thing to watch. Because of competition in the political arena, politicians are encouraged to make visible improvements to the country in an effort to gain voters' (10) _____. This in the end can benefit everyone. Finally, competition in industry usually brings about lower prices, which is undoubtedly (11) _____ to consumers.

To (12) _____, competition has both good and bad points. Although it can result in dishonesty and exploitation, its benefits outweigh its (13) _____ and have a positive effect on many aspects of our lives. Moreover, the competitive spirit is always with us and is difficult to control, (14) _____ hard people try.

 原來如此

1.	**aganist**	由此句句首 However 得知此句和上一句是相反的觀點，第一句指競爭是 driving force behind improvements (進步背後的驅動力量)，第二句則是反面觀點，因此選 against (*prep.*) 反對。
2.	**do**	do without... 沒有…也行，cannot do without 沒有…不行。
3.	**encourage**	競爭會助長 (encourage) 欺瞞 (dishonesty)。
4.	**improve**	運動員服藥是要改善 (improve) 他們場上的表現。
5.	**known**	someone be known to... 據說某人會…。
6.	**lie**	由之前的 untruthful 得知此格選 lie to get votes (說謊以得到選票)。
7.	**industry**	由 produce more goods 得知以下作者由工業 (industry) 觀念來談。
8.	**wages**	剝削 (exploit) 勞工是指「工作時間長但工資 (wages) 低」。
9.	**effort**	make the greatest effort 非常努力
10.	**support**	政客努力 (in an effort to) 獲得選民的支持 (support)。
11.	**beneficial**	企業競爭對顧客 (consumers) 是有益的 (beneficial)。
12.	**conclude**	to conclude (總之) 是常用在結語處的承轉語。
13.	**drawbacks**	好處大於壞處 (drawbacks)；outweigh 比…重要。
14.	**however**	此處 however 是從屬連接詞，however hard = no matter how hard。

寫作要點

議論文及短文解析

A. 議論文 Argumentation

議論文是以說理的方式說服讀者相信其論點。例如此篇文章的寫作目的就是「說服讀者」，雖然競爭有利有弊，但利大於弊。

議論文寫作時的要點：(1) 論點要清楚明確。
(2) 推論要層次分明。
(3) 說理要強而有力。

論點可以用列舉事實、提出證據 (包括統計數字、研究報告、引用權威人士的話等)，以重要順序，或者以比較 (comparison) 或對比 (contrast) 的方式安排。

B. Cloze 短文解析

1. 引言 (**Introduction**)：

包括了很清楚的兩個對立的想法 (ideas)，正面的是 However, competition has long

been the driving force behind improvements.... 反面的是 Much can be said against the desire to come first.。而且還引用了 Bernard Hunt 這位記者的話來強調不是他個人的說法而已。

2. 主體 (**Body**)：

作者必須依據引言採用正反對立的要點安排。作者採用的是第一段論述反面，第二段論述正面，至此讀者應該猜到了作者偏向正面，即「競爭的好處大於壞處」。因為在論述的過程中總是把重要的放在後面，而且第二段緊接第三段，在邏輯上更有「連貫性」。以下列出主體部分的要點大綱對了解作者的思考邏輯更有幫助。

I. Disadvantages (A) Athletes—take drugs
  (B) Politicians—lie to get votes
  (C) Industry—exploit employees
II. Advantages (A) Athletes—make the game exciting to watch
  (B) Politicians—make visible improvements to the country
  (C) Industry—benefit consumers

3. 結語 (**Conclusion**)：

作者提出其一番論述之後的結論：競爭優點大於缺點，而且有其正面影響。何況人一直都有競爭心理，很難控制不去競爭 (its benefits outweigh its drawbacks and have a positive effect on many aspects of our lives; the competitive spirit is always with us and is difficult to control)。

※本篇短文可以學到：

(1) 議論文常用的手法：
  引言部分提出正反對立的看法，主體部分做正反面的論述，然後做出結論。
(2) 主體部分作者採用的安排要點的方式：
  在第二段 (壞處) 及第三段 (好處) 分別就 athletes、politicians 及 industry 三方面討論。

Extra

(1) 表示比較或對比的承轉語

like, unlike, likewise, similarly, however, nevertheless, nonetheless, although, while, but, yet, in spite of/despite, by comparison, on the contrary, on the other hand

(2) 表示結論的承轉語

to conclude, to summarize, to sum up, in brief, in short, in conclusion, in sum, on the whole, by and large

寫作練習

A. 電腦影響你的生活有多大呢？你交網友嗎？你去網咖嗎？

請參考以下範例之後，以 Computers—Productive or Destructive 或 My Opinions on Making Key Pals 為題寫一篇 120 字至 150 字左右的作文。

Should Teenagers Be Forbidden to Surf the Net at Internet Café

Internet cafés are becoming another hotspot for teenagers almost everywhere in Taiwan. Isn't it a good place to go if teenagers don't have computers with high-speed Internet connection at home?

Some people suggest that the government should enact laws or regulations which forbid teenage children to go to an Internet café. They worry that these children might get bad influences, such as violence, pornography, from the Internet, because they might not be under any supervision as they are in school or at home. They also worry that staying at Internet cafés till midnight would interfere with their schoolwork.

In my opinion, if any supervision or guidance is necessary, it should be offered by parents, not by any regulation proposed by the government. A good education begins at home. It is parents that should shoulder the responsibility of educating their children. Staying there till midnight or even all night should be restricted by parents, not by the government. And it can't be denied that the cyberworld is just like the real world. If parents agree that to teach their children to distinguish what should be done from what should not be done is the way to help them live in the world, why not in the cyberworld? Very often too strict regulations just push curious teenagers to embrace it, not to keep away from it.

So if under the guidance of parents, teenagers can have the access to Internet cafés, especially for academics or a little entertainment. I do not agree to the suggestion that teenagers should be forbidden to surf the Net at Internet cafés.

B. 請以下列題目練習作文

1. 以 "Why I Like to Read Comic Books/Play Computer Games/Sing at KTV" 或 "Why I Need a CD Walkman/High-priced Sports Shoes/a New PC" 為題，說服你的父母相信你需要這些東西。

2. 以 "A Letter to a Runaway" 為題，勸蹺家的孩子回家。

NOTE

A Letter Home

June 10, 2006

Dear Family,

I hope everyone at home is healthy and doing well. I am having a wonderful time now, although __1__ I had a bit of "culture shock." Initially everything seemed new and exciting, but once the __2__ wore off things were very frustrating. Some days I didn't even want to leave my room, and I got very irritated whenever I had trouble __3__ things that are very easy at home but tough over here. Things are getting better though and I'm starting to __4__.

Classes have also been a challenge. Professors always assign a lot of reading, and __5__ up with it all is very difficult. Prioritizing is also not easy. Sometimes a professor asks all the students to know an article inside and out, but __6__ times a professor doesn't even mention a particular reading.

Another challenge has been fitting in. Although people are very nice, it's tough to __7__ how people feel or what they think. I want to fit in and learn how to do things, but I also don't want to stop being a Taiwanese! There are several Chinese students in my classes, and we help one another with the assignments and __8__ together on the weekends.

I've also been to a truly amazing place, New York City. With immigrants from almost every country in the world, it is one of the most racially __9__ cities, __10__ it a great place to eat and shop. And you can't imagine how excited I was to watch a Major League Baseball game at Yankee Stadium.

I can't wait to see you all.

Love,

Iris

P.S. Thanks for calling last weekend! It was great to hear from you.

_____ 1. (A) for good   (B) at first   (C) firstly   (D) lastly

_____ 2. (A) novelty   (B) shock   (C) crisis   (D) panic

_____ 3. (A) into   (B) with   (C) in   (D) of

_____ 4. (A) approve   (B) tolerate   (C) adjust   (D) resist

_____ 5. (A) fitting   (B) putting   (C) lining   (D) keeping

_____ 6. (A) another   (B) other   (C) the other   (D) all other

_____ 7. (A) speak   (B) tell   (C) read   (D) see

_____ 8. (A) hang out   (B) sneak at   (C) get through   (D) run out

_____ 9. (A) biased   (B) focused   (C) diverse   (D) tense

_____ 10. (A) to make   (B) making   (C) to cause   (D) causing

UNIT 30

NOTE

 原來如此

1. **B** 過去式 had 是線索，空格會是個可以表達「過去時間的副詞」at first (起初)。(A) 永遠 (C) 第一 (D) 最後。

2. **A** 形容詞 new 是線索，此格重複用字，是其同義但不同詞性的字 novelty (新鮮)。(B) 震驚 (C) 危機 (D) 恐慌

3. **B** have trouble with... 有…的煩惱／困擾。

4. **C** 事情好轉也開始適應 (adjust) 了。(A) 贊同 (B) 容忍 (D) 抵抗

5. **D** keep up with... 跟上／趕得上…

6. **C** sometimes (有時候) 搭配 other times (其他時候) 來表達「一般狀況」。

7. **B** tell + wh-clause or wh-+ to+ V 表達知道…而其他選項沒有這用法

8. **A** hang out (外出閒逛) (B) 偷偷摸摸溜走 (C) 穿過度過困難 (D) 耗盡用完

9. **C** 線索在此空格後的文意 with immigrants from almost every country in the world(來自各國的移民…)，可以得知此格選 racially diverse (種族多元的)。(A) 種族偏見的 (D) 緊張的。

10. **B** make + O + OC；表示同時發生的動作用分詞 making (參考 Unit 3 句式分析 1)。

 寫作練習

如何寫私人信件及電子郵件 (How to Write Personal Letters and Email)

A. 私人信件 (包括寫給親人朋友的信，感謝卡，邀請函)
   (本章的克漏字文章就是一封寫給家人信件的範例)

   私人信件的格式 (**Format for Personal Letters**)：
   (1) 信件右上角的日期 (Date)，例如：April 4, 2006
   (2) 左邊日期下一行的稱謂 (Salutation)，例如 Dear Uncle Jim, Dear John，等等。
   (3) 信件的主體 (Body)，位置在稱謂下一行。(寫法說明在下方)
   (4) 結尾敬辭 (Complimentary Close)，位置在主體右下方，例如寫給朋友用的 Sincerely yours, Best wishes, 寫給家人則用 Love,。
   (5) 下一行與結尾部份齊頭的簽名 (Signature)。
   (6) 附言 (Postscript) 是如果寫完後還要再補充一點時用的，先寫 P.S. 然後寫出要補充的內容。

信件的主體的寫法

(1) 信件開頭就像見面時一樣會寒暄一番，有以下幾種情形：

表達問候的：How's everything? What's up? How's your life? How's school?

表達感謝的：Thank you so much for your gift. I'm so happy to hear from you.

敘述久未聯絡或見面的：I haven't heard from you for a long time.

(2) 問候之後，就依照你寫信的目的，以很輕鬆語氣寫出自己的近況、發生的事情、你的看法、或者你的感謝。

(3) 結尾通常都寫一些表達思念、再聯絡或提醒之類的文字：

Take care. Please write back as soon as possible. Keep in touch. Miss you a lot.

信封的格式：

B. 電子郵件 (email)

電子郵件沒有傳統書信那麼正式，在遣詞用字和風格上通常不那麼嚴謹。

撰寫步驟：

(1) 在撰寫郵件 (new message or compose) 視窗上，會出現三個重要的部分：

To: emily@hotmail.com
CC:
Subject: Re about the class reunion in November
Dear Emily, Thanks for telling me we'll have a class reunion in November. I'm working in New York City now. I'm not sure if I can have some days off to go back to Taiwan then, but I will write to you if I can make it. Best, Wendy

(a) To： 輸入收件者的地址 (receiver's email address)

(b) CC： 輸入收附件者的地址 (CC 指 carbon copy)，如果不寄附件，可空白。

(c) Subject： 輸入信件內容主旨。主旨不必寫完整的句子，原則是要很簡短清楚，讓對方一眼就知道內容是什麼。例如：party; reunion; thanks; about admission.... 等。

(d) 郵件：在 Subject: 下方的框框內寫下郵件內容。(有些人省略稱謂和署名。但基於禮貌，寫給長輩的時候最好保留。另外，若寄件人或收件人和別人共用 email address 時，稱謂和署名也最好不要省略。)

寫作練習

A. 請重新閱讀 Unit 21 的克漏字短文，假設你是 Mullins 的鄰居，明天他就要判決了。寫一封信給他告訴他你對這件事的看法，在情感上給予支持 .。

B. 寫一張卡片祝福你的朋友要畢業了。

C. 發一封 Email 給你的朋友，謝謝她送你禮物。

參考範例

A.

July 20, 2001

Dear Mr. Mullins,

I am so sorry to hear about the verdict and what you had gone through. It was cruel to see your beloved wife suffering like that. You must have struggled these through years.

It is also cruel that they are going to put you in prison for 25 years. I think this sentence is too harsh. The jury may not want people to think it is right to kill a sick family member even if he/she has lain in bed for a long time. However, any family member would be tortured by the pain his/her beloved experienced. Should this become a reason for punishment? I still believe there must be a better way to solve the dilemma; if not, we need to think about it now.

Sincerely yours,

Iris Cheng

108課綱、各類英檢考試 適用

Cloze & Writing Practice

克漏字與寫作練習

解析本

李文玲　編著

三民書局

TRANSLATION

Unit 1

在 9 至 18 歲這段年紀之間，你會經歷一連串生理上的改變，我們稱之為青春期。青春期有時會產生一些問題，包括了皮膚問題，令人煩惱的毛髮狀況和情緒起伏不定。有時候你會覺得非常快樂與自信，有時候你又覺得對自我及外表沒有把握。

為了應付這些變化，你必須保持身體健康。如果你的身體狀況良好，你會覺得精力充沛並充滿自信，能夠處理應付日常生活中的起起伏伏。身體健康狀況會影響你對待自己外表的感覺。你的健康狀況由你的外表展現，一個快樂健康的人擁有好的肌膚和毛髮，眼中還會閃爍著光芒。

良好的健康狀況使你更能抵抗疾病和傳染病。它也能夠幫助保護你免於某些成年期的疾病，像是心臟病。當你還年輕時，這些長期的好處看起來似乎不重要，但是健康生活的好處你一定馬上感覺得到。

Unit 2

世界上每個文化都會有迷信。即使非常理性和科學的社會有時也會有點迷信。舉例來說，美國是一個在科學和科技上都非常先進的國家。但是即使在美國社會，人們有時候也會迷信。他們認為「十三」是個不吉利的數字。所以我們很難發現 13 層的建築物或是門牌為 13 號的住宅。當 13 號碰到星期五，你可以想像他們作何感受，很多人認為這天不吉利。

除了有關數字的迷信之外，美國人往往認為打破鏡子是很不吉利的。如果有人打破鏡子，他或她將遭遇七年的不幸。此外，他們總是避免從梯子下走過，以免為自己帶來厄運。黑貓也是不吉利的，尤其當牠們從人類的面前走過。很久以前，人們相信黑貓其實是巫婆所偽裝的。

有些迷信行為已經變成風俗習慣。當有人打噴嚏時，他們會說：「願上帝保佑你」。過去，人們相信打噴嚏時，靈魂會從軀體跑出。被賜福是為了保護自己以免失去靈魂。

Unit 3

位在東京鬧區的「機器人購物商店」是世界上第一家沒有人類員工的商店。機器人每天 24 小時工作，服務走進商店的顧客。

「機器人購物商店」就像一台巨大的自動販賣機。顧客們進入商店並觀看陳列櫃。他們在訂單上寫下他們想要物品的號碼。接著他們把號碼輸入一台類似自動提款機的機器。然後，一架叫 Robo 的機器人開始作業。

Robo 看起來像一個裝有輪子的桶子。它迅速地在店內四處移動，挑選商品然後把它們放到購物籃中。Robo 總是會先挑選最大的物品。如果你買了一台新的烤麵包機，Robo 不會將它放在新鮮的壽司上面。

「機器人購物商店」販賣許多人們每天要買的東西：從食品、飲料到家用物品、雜誌以及化妝品。它也販賣很多其他商品，像是昂貴的手錶和香水。「機器人購物商店」就像是一臺自動販賣機，只是大多了。許多人認為在那裡購物很有趣，而且價錢也比較便宜，因為商店不用付機器人薪水。

Unit 4

希區考克也許可算是至今最出名的電影導演；他的電影之如此受歡迎，是因為它們能引發電影觀眾心中強烈的情感。在不同的鏡頭之下，觀眾常常隨之尖叫、大笑、顫慄、或是甚至閉上眼睛。

希區考克是個使觀眾和劇中人物覺得焦慮的專家，他的人物常常身陷於他們無法理解的危險處境中；但在這些鏡頭中，希區考克會讓觀眾知道危險是什麼，觀眾想警告劇中人物要小心，但是劇中人物當然無法注意到這些警告。

在大部分的懸疑電影中，危險的事通常發生在黑暗、可怕的地方；但是在希區考克的電影中，不好的事通常發生在明亮且「安全」的地方。舉例來說，在電影「鳥」中，一個女人安靜地坐在靠近學校的公園裡，她不知道那些鳥正設法要佔領她的城鎮。她看到一隻黑鳥停在兒童遊戲的方格鐵架上。再看時，上千隻鳥已經聚集在她周圍；不久，這些鳥攻擊她和學童。

希區考克的另一個特色是將幽默放入可怕的鏡頭；他知道當人們被驚嚇時會莞爾一笑，電影中的幽默會使觀眾看電影時覺得更加緊張。

Unit 5

根據聯合國的統計，全球有超過一億無家可歸的人。他們住哪呢？就在像是廢棄的建築物、收容所、公車和火車站、地下鐵以及馬路上。紐約和倫敦這些大城市幾乎無法應付這些大量的街頭流浪漢。

要估計出這些無家可歸者的確切數字是不可能的，因為他們的狀況都不同。比如說，有時候人們因為火災或是風災而暫時流離失所；有時候人們因為付不起房租而被迫離家；而有些人可能已流浪街頭數年了。要去算他們到底有多少人並不容易，要去描述一個典型的無家可歸者也不簡單，因為他們會因時因地而異。

造成無家可歸的原因有哪些？對某些人來說，就是純粹無法負擔住宅的費用；很多無家可歸者皆已失業且相當窮困。還有許多人有嗑藥和酗酒問題；有些人因為家裡狀況不好而離家。有些則有精神上的疾病，離開醫院後沒地方可去，他們沒有家人也沒有任何人可以求助。

為了解決問題已有一些建議，但是要解決當前的問題確實還需要點時間。

Unit 6

電腦在我們每天的生活中很有幫助。但你能想像它們當起媒人來了嗎？近來它們已經使尋找合適的另一半變得容易許多。在全球各地，電腦擇友已成為新興的行業。人們的時間愈來愈少，要求愈來愈高，大部分的人找不出時間去認識新朋友，也擔不起盲目約會的風險。所以，只要一些合理的費用，將你的個人資料，連同你的好惡輸入一套軟體中，它會列出一串可能與你速配的名字，接下來你只需要打電話就行了。

假如你願意多花點錢，可以製作你的個人影片，在影片中你可以介紹自己及談談你欣賞的類型。影片會被轉檔存入電腦中，人們可從螢幕上選擇他們的另一半。如果你有個人電腦，你可以透過網路進入這個系統。額外付費的話，你可以很舒服地在家看到男主角或女主角的影像；如果一切順利的話，最後你可以邀請你的電腦擔任婚禮上的男儐相或女儐相。

Unit 7

美國農業部的統計資料顯示，過去在晚餐中最受歡迎的紅肉再也不是美國人的最愛了；反之，雞肉、火雞肉和魚肉已愈來愈受歡迎。近年來這些食物的銷售量已大幅提昇，這也許是因為意識到高膽固醇或動物性脂肪食物所帶來的危險。醫生們相信膽固醇對人類是一項威脅。

美國人也為了因應不同的情況而改變飲食型態。他們知道哪些食物可以增進體能或是幫助減重，哪些能使他們在會議中保持清醒，哪些可以培養浪漫情緒。舉例來說，美國人選擇含醣的義大利麵、水果和蔬菜來供給身體活動所需的能量。成人會選擇富含纖維的食物來當作早餐，像是麵包和穀片；而午餐則吃沙拉，好為接下來的商務約會做準備。不過，若是羅曼蒂克的晚餐，則會選擇蝦類和龍蝦。這些觀念有些是以正確營養觀念為根據，有些則否。

美國人對於營養的認知，以及不斷改變的口味和需求，致使他們為了健康，為了樂趣，或單純只是為了好吃而選擇多樣化的食物。

Unit 8

雖然肢體語言在動物的交配儀式中是很重要的一部分，它在許多其他場合中也是不可缺少的溝通方式。許多動物擁有問候的方式。當同類動物在野地相遇時，牠們不確定面對的是敵人或是朋友，所以牠們透過謹慎的問候方式來確定對方沒有攻擊自己的企圖。

另外有些動物有獨特的訊號來警告同類週遭是否有危險；在北美洲有一種白尾巴的鹿，當牠受到驚嚇時，會筆直翹起尾巴逃跑，其他的鹿看到這個警告訊息時就會知道牠們也該逃跑。

蜜蜂則使用肢體語言來傳達訊息，牠們在夏天採集花粉和花蜜以製造蜂蜜。如果一隻蜜蜂發現一大片的花叢，牠會飛回蜂巢，以8字型飛舞著，一邊扭動和搖動牠的身體。當其他蜜蜂看到這些動作時，牠們就會知道花叢在哪兒，然後飛出去採集花蜜。

就像人類一樣，動物也透過臉部表情來表達牠們的情緒和感受。當黑猩猩受到驚嚇或是激動時，會張大嘴巴並露出牙齒；牠們打招呼時常突出嘴唇來；而當想讓自己看起來凶惡時，牠們會緊閉雙唇。

Unit 9

一百年前，曬成古銅色的肌膚並不流行。曬黑的皮膚通常表示一個人在太陽底下工作。農人、建築工人和牛仔都有古銅色皮膚；接受較高教育的人從事室內工作，所以他們的皮膚比較不容易曬黑。事實上，很多人試著保護他們的皮膚避免日曬，希望能讓他人認為是受過教育的知識份子。男人戴寬緣的帽子，女人則攜帶繡花洋傘以隔離陽光。

在20世紀後期，曬黑的皮膚變得非常流行，各地的年輕人坐在在太陽底下數小時，翻轉各種角度希望膚色曬得均勻；曬黑的皮膚在當時蔚為風行，因為只有有錢的人才有閒待在太陽底下什麼事也不做！

但陽光會造成皮膚細胞的病變，亞利桑那州和其他日曬強烈的地方，像是昆士蘭和澳洲，都有許多癌症案例。皮膚癌是種皮膚異常細胞失去控制生長的嚴重疾病。所以，人們今天會保護皮膚避免日曬。醫生建議了幾個方法來保護皮膚。

一、在早上10點和下午3點間，別曬太陽，這是一天之中陽光最毒的時候。

二、使用具保護作用的防曬乳液，它的防曬係數至少要15以上。

三、穿著合適的服裝，寬緣的帽子、長袖襯衫、長褲和長裙都可以保護皮膚防止日曬。

Unit 10

龐大的鐵達尼號在1912年4月10日從南安普敦航向紐約，船上有1316名乘客及891名船員。在當時，她不僅是史上最大的船艦，也因為她有16個防水隔間，而被譽為是永遠不沉的。即使其中兩個進水了，她仍然能夠漂浮。但人們將會永遠記得這艘船艦的沉船悲劇，因為在她的處女航中，便駛向幽暗的海底深處，也帶走了許多生命。

4月14日時，正當鐵達尼號穿越北大西洋冰冷的海域時，瞭望員突然發現一塊巨大的冰山，在發出警報後，這艘巨大船艦迅速急轉以避免正面撞擊，但仍然撞上了冰山。突然，從下面傳出震動的聲音，船長走下去看看發生了什麼事；震動聲是如此微弱，沒有人會想到這艘船已遭損。令船長恐懼的是，他明白鐵達尼很快地就要沉了，她16個防水隔艙已有五個完全進水！船長宣佈棄船，上百人跳入冰冷的海水中。由於沒有足夠的救生艇，1500人就此喪生。

Unit 11

在許多文化中，人們以圖畫和花紋來妝繪身體。有時候會用能洗掉的染料彩繪身體；而其它形式的人體彩繪，像是刺青，則會永久留在身上。人們常常為了特定目的而彩繪身體，其目的反映在他們使用的圖案種類上。

北美洲的原住民普遍使用人體彩繪。當戰士們準備戰鬥時，他們會用顯眼大膽的圖案。他們使用紅色線條、面部塗黑，並將眼睛周圍塗成白色圓圈來強調臉部。這些圖案使這些戰士們看起來兇猛且具攻擊性。其他民族也使用戰鬥彩妝。當羅馬人侵略英國時，他們發現這些不列顛人在上戰場前會使用靛青染料塗在身上。

人體彩繪也可以用在戰爭之外的場合。澳洲的原住民在「科洛波里」（狂歡會）上常用明顯的白色標記彩繪身體──所謂「科洛波里」是種人們跳舞唱歌的特殊聚會。

紐西蘭的毛利人使用刺青來裝飾身體，這種永久的身體標記顯示出個人的社會地位。越重要的人身上的刺青也越多，有些酋長和國王的臉上就完全佈滿了刺青。

Unit 12

每天早上數以百萬的人心不甘情不願地起床，隨便套上衣服，然後拿起早報，睡眼惺忪地看看報紙上的漫畫。

諷刺漫畫反映了時代和人們的憂愁煩惱，也給人們一個嘲笑自己和類似情境的機會。它也取笑人們自找麻煩，像是為了買哪一個牌子的車而苦惱；經濟不景氣的時候，人們想歸咎於某人，諷刺漫畫提供了代罪羔羊；它也幫助人們在笑不出來的情況中幽默一下。舉例來說，諷刺漫畫也許會表示一國的政府要為不景氣的經濟負責，並顯示出政府領導者是一群幼稚可笑的人物，這使人們對所處情況較能釋懷。

諷刺漫畫也使人們嘲笑自己的煩惱。常常手足無措的年輕人可以會心一笑看待自己的笨拙，缺乏孩子關心的老人可以暗笑自己的孤獨，考前臨時抱佛腳的學生可以譏笑自己的焦慮。在諷刺漫畫裡，每個人的苦惱都畫成比生命還重要。而這些之所以會讓人覺得好笑，也許是因為當真實的事情以不真實的方式呈現時，幽默隨之而生。

Unit 13

澳洲塔斯馬尼亞省有項普遍的嗜好─打毛衣，但可不是普通的毛衣！而是整個塔斯馬尼亞島都有志願者為企鵝編織的迷你毛衣！

企鵝屬於不會飛翔的鳥類，棲息在南半球，包括塔斯馬尼亞，澳洲南方的島嶼，以魚類為生，雖然築巢和產卵都在陸上，不過多半時間都待在水中。企鵝飛不起來，但牠們的羽毛很特殊，在冰冷的水中既可以保暖，又具有防水的功能。但當企鵝受到原油外洩波及時，油漬會阻塞牠們的羽毛，再也無法保持溫暖，而且牠們只要試圖清理自己，就會將羽毛上的油舔食而下，此舉會毒害企鵝，導致牠們病重乃至於死亡。

企鵝穿著毛衣時能保持溫暖乾燥，免於誤食羽毛上的油料，去年塔斯馬尼亞以及來自世界各地的志願者，共編織了一萬五千件的毛衣，存放起來以備嚴重的原油外洩時使用。

你若熱衷編織且願意付出，網路上可以找到企鵝毛衣的圖樣，毛衣必須用純羊毛編製，且須以手工加以編織緊實，鬆散的編織會造成毛衣出現縫隙，企鵝的喙或羽翼則可能因此勾住。毛衣的顏色不要緊，但通常編織的人會選擇最吸引人的樣式，即使是「最趕流行」的企鵝也適合，而穿上條紋毛衣的企鵝特別可愛。通常，牠們看上去就像穿著黑色搭白色的正式晚宴服(母企鵝亦然)，但穿上這些毛衣，看起來就有如穿便服一般了！

Unit 14

姓氏起初用於區分同名的人，我們的姓氏有著不同的來源，大多數的姓氏都是從共同的來源演變而來，舉凡職業、住所、父名、或特徵。

姓氏源自職業的歷史已達數世紀之久，從事木工者姓 Carpenter (意為木匠)；泥水匠姓 Mason (砌磚匠)；製造木桶的人就稱之為 Cooper (箍桶匠)；幾乎每個村莊都有一位打鐵師傅，因此幾乎每個村莊都有人姓 Smith (鐵匠)。

許多其他的姓氏由住所產生，若某人住在山上，就成了 Overhill；若居住在溪邊，就可能稱之為 Brook；而你也可以從跟地理有關的字眼來辨別一個字是否與住所有關，例如以 hill、wood 或 brook 結尾的字都是如此，但也不是所有的字尾都這麼容易認出，姓氏中以 ton、ham 或 stead 結尾的字代表農田；而 leigh 或 ley 結尾的字代表拓墾地。

然而，也有別的姓氏來自父親的名字，比方說，一個人姓 Jackson，代表他是 Jack 後人，而姓 Peterson 則為 Peter 後人。最後，許多姓氏的出現，是因為身體上的特徵，假如一個人身材矮小，很可能就被稱為 Short，反之如果很高的話，就可能被稱為 Longfellow；至於 Kennedy 這個姓在塞爾提克語中意為「ugly head」；至於一個人若有動物的特性，則可能會被冠上如 Fox 之類的姓氏，前提是這人要夠狡猾。

讀到這裡，以後你聽到一個姓氏時，就更能了解其由來了，甚至還能告訴對方關於他祖先的二三事。

Unit 15

查沃斯莊園位於英格蘭德貝郡，坐擁千畝的的公園和農地，終年都是遊憩的好去處，但隨著季節有著不同的變化。春天時，農地裡的動物如豬、牛、綿羊、雞和山羊繁衍後代，你可以來趟春日森林健行，去觀賞牠們，順便欣賞野花和吐露新芽的樹木。

到了夏天有特別的動物展覽，以及「認識動物」的系列活動，其中包括擠牛乳和擠羊乳的現場表演，還可撫摸和輕擁小羊和雛雞，只要天氣回暖，還可搭牽引機穿過史丹德森林區。不過只要兩、三個月之後就是秋天了，樹葉即轉色從樹梢落下，森林步道正是欣賞秋天絢爛多彩的最佳路徑。

冬天比其他季節來得寒冷，活動也移到室內，有間工藝品小木屋每天都開放，方便你製作具有鄉村風格的耶誕裝飾品和卡片，你也可以參與室內的耶誕說故事、表演和歌唱活動，天氣不錯的話，仍可到室外搭牽引機繞行農場。

公園寬廣開闊的空間全年開放，公園各處和流經公園的德文特河濱可供步行、野餐或玩耍。公園的設計要回溯到 1760 年代，如今已是英國最優美且最悠久的人造景觀。與農地不同之處在於，公園是一處未開發的地方，白天任何時候都可供人任意走動，公園和花園各處都點綴著傳統與現代的雕刻品，而放眼望去還有小型湖泊和蜿蜒走道穿插其間，以這種方式享受大好的英倫鄉間風情真是太怡人了。

Unit 16

你喜歡食物帶有辣味嗎?沒問題,只要拿起胡椒在菜餚上灑幾下,多麼簡單啊!但是幾千年前,要讓食物能刺激味蕾並不是那麼簡單。我們今天習以為常的黑胡椒,其珍貴程度在古代讓人難以想像。事實上若沒有黑胡椒,這世界將完全改觀。

黑胡椒的來源是胡椒樹,這種植物會長出胡椒莓,當果實半熟時會在太陽底下乾燥,最終轉變成黑色。磨成粉後,就是餐桌上看到的胡椒。過程聽起來不複雜,但在多年以前黑胡椒只生長在印度,所以它必須長途運送,才能抵達歐洲人和非洲人的手上,這也使得這種香料異常珍貴。

黑胡椒在從前有「黑金」之稱,就連埃及法老拉美西斯二世木乃伊的鼻孔中都有其蹤跡,其價值之高可見一斑。此外還謠傳匈奴王阿提拉汗願意停止進攻羅馬,只要羅馬人願意獻上一頓的黑胡椒。這也不難想見,歐、亞各國間的胡椒及其他香料買賣不僅是樁好生意,更促成了新領土的發現,以及大城市如威尼斯的建立。

黑胡椒的價格最終在西元 1600 年代走下坡,當時船隻可以直接簡易地跨洲航行;而今,胡椒雖然不貴,但仍有其療效。就我們所知,黑胡椒助消化,因為其辛辣感會告訴胃部要分泌一定量的胃酸,將我們吃下肚的食物分解,換句話說,食物不會待在我們體內過久,因為如果這樣的話,我們可能會胃痛或消化不良。

Unit 17

你曾在課堂上打瞌睡嗎?或是曾被老師怒氣沖天喚醒嗎?這種事的發生頻率是否愈來愈高呢?在學校睡著了可能是因為你晚上熬夜,也有可能是老師巨細靡遺的歷史課所致,但近來的研究顯示有其他更確切的原因在起作用,而你也決不是一個人在打瞌睡。

一項調查指出,美國青少年中只有百分之 20 睡眠充足。有百分之 17 的人會失眠,也就是說即便他們想入睡卻不可得。無疑地,睡眠不足在許多方面困擾青少年的生活,會造成他們容易焦慮、學業低落,以及許許多多的健康問題,像是糖尿病、心臟病、肥胖等,每晚至少有九個小時的睡眠對青少年來說極為重要。那麼為何有這麼多人有晚上睡覺的問題或白天無法保持清醒呢?

當然,也有一般的因素。學生容易有許多功課,也常與朋友通電話和去玩樂,這些全都進行到凌晨。研究人員也提出電子產品是造成睡眠不足的一大因素。因為手機、電腦、iPod 和電視等過度刺激青年年的大腦,以致他們難以入眠。此外在青少年到達青春期時,褪黑激素(一種有助睡眠的荷爾蒙)在凌晨一點左右分泌。這表示青少年將「想睡覺」的時間延後,因而導致睡眠不足。

青少年睡眠時數不足應如何改善呢?或許他們試著白天的時候運動、每天按時就寢,並在睡前關閉所有電子產品以讓一切放鬆安靜。

Unit 18

奧比斯 (ORBIS) 為一非營利、非政府的國際組織,為預防失明而提供免費的醫療與訓練,其最著名之處要屬一架由 DC-10 型飛機改裝的「眼科飛行醫院」。奧比斯不僅在紐約成立總部,在休士頓、倫敦、香港與台北等地亦設有辦事處。

台灣之所以獲選為奧比斯在亞洲的第二個辦事處,是因為台灣擁有高水準的眼科醫學和經濟上的優異成果。2001 年時,台灣奧比斯登記成為國際性的非政府發展機構。

台灣奧比斯以台北為根據地,由常務董事,同時也是台北醫學大學眼科教授的蔡瑞芳醫師領軍,在他的領導之下,台灣奧比斯的任務包括:為國內學童舉辦護眼教育計畫、為國內及海外社區進行視力保健活動,並支援國際奧比斯的活動。

在這眾多活動當中,台灣奧比斯的志工於 2005 年 7 月飛往中國新疆,進行為期一周的兒童眼科訓練和義診活動。由於新疆當地日照強烈，不少居民罹患青光眼和白內障，但因當地經濟條件不佳，許多家庭無法負擔適當治療的費用，因此台灣奧比斯的計畫造福了許多人。

台灣奧比斯的醫生曾接過一項個案，是一名叫做穆拉迪格的五歲男童，他出生即患有青光眼，但有幸於 2001 年接受美國奧比斯的義診手術，挽救了右眼視力；在這計畫過程中，台灣奧比斯的醫師群恢復男童的左眼視力，如今他已能清楚見物。

在國際奧比斯與國內銀行、企業、社團及個人的資金挹注之下，台灣奧比斯已能持續地運作，然而，台灣奧比斯仍有一項必須持之以恆的活動，就是喚醒意識並且籌募經費，用以根除不必要的失明，並有更多事項有待努力，好讓「眼科飛行醫院」展翅高飛。

Unit 19

A. 營養的搭配能影響我們的健康狀況，沒有一種營養可以單獨產生作用；舉例來說，需要鈣質才能建造強壯的骨骼，但那只是開始階段，沒有維他命 D 的話，鈣就無法被人體吸收。另一個例子是蛋白質，蛋白質構成細胞及其周圍的液體，然而，還需要維他命 C 來幫助製造細胞間的液體；沒有維他命 C 的話，蛋白質就沒辦法作用了。

B. 大部分的學生因為三個理由而不同意穿著制服。首先，當你必須和其他人穿著一樣時，你就沒有機會展現你自己的衣著品味；再者，看起來窮酸的人即使穿著制服通常看起來一樣窮酸，而且你總是可以分辨出誰來自貧窮家庭，因為他們的制服沒有別人的新且不合身；最後，大部分學生不喜歡制服的主要原因是：許多學校都選用很糟糕的顏色和款式，一點都不適合年輕人。

Unit 20

近來科技的發展改變了我們的教育體制。其中一項對學生有顯著影響的就是電視。幼童在一兩歲的時候就開始看像芝麻街之類的幼教節目。這些節目以寓教於樂的方式來介紹數字、字母及簡單的算術。針對初等及中等教育的學生則設計有數學、科學及閱讀之類的課後節目。有些大學對電視課程也給學分。學生可以去教室收看教授的電視教學，或是待在家裡看特別設計的電視節目。

另一項對教育有重大影響的，就是日趨重要的教具：個人電腦。從學前到成人階段，有許多適用學校的每個科目、主題及各種程度的軟體程式。學生喜歡用電腦，因為他們可以靠自己操作及依自己的步調。而許多軟體程式以遊戲的形式來設計。這些程式因兼具娛樂性及教育性而受歡迎。此外，許多學生從線上服務及網際網路上獲得資訊，用文書處理程式去寫作業。隨著現代科技的進步，學生使用的工具也與時俱進。

Unit 21

由七男五女組成的陪審團今天做成判決，78 歲的安德魯・穆林斯由於謀殺他 80 歲妻子艾荻絲，而被判有罪。六個禮拜前，穆林斯因謀殺而受審。

這樁悲劇發生在 8 月 10 日晚上，在穆林斯家位於龐斯頓灘小鎮的家裡。那天早晨，他飽受肺癌及老人癡呆症所折磨的妻子，以空洞的眼神看著他，還問他究竟是誰。那天傍晚，她痛苦不堪並不斷嚷著：「救救我，救救我。」當天晚上，當她睡在沙發上時，穆林斯把槍指著她的頭，開槍殺了她；然後他打電話報警並告訴警方他做了什麼。兩天後他被控謀殺。

在審判中穆林斯說道：「我所殺的女人不是我妻子，而是一個痛苦的軀體與沒有記憶的心靈；我不認為我犯下了謀殺罪。」

幾名證人被傳喚去提供證詞。有些鄰居說穆林斯太太喜歡外出，總是面帶微笑，會化點妝；醫生說她病得很重。朋友說穆林斯先生很愛他的太太。但是最後，陪審團達成有罪的判決，他們與檢察官意見一致，那是謀殺罪。

明天法官將會判決，依據法律穆林斯至少坐 25 年的牢。那表示他到 103 歲時才會出獄。

Unit 22

中國古老的風水之學已流傳至美國！風水是居家、辦公及傢俱擺設的學問，以求與自然和諧，相信風水的人認為這有助於我們的健康、財運和幸福。美國人對風水抱著極大的熱忱，目前幾乎在各個書店皆可購得英文的風水書籍，有也網站介紹風水，甚至美國的大學也熱衷開課教授風水學。

風水何以能在美國造成熱潮？這麼說吧，許多美國人身居擁擠繁忙的都市，遠離大自然且生活步調快速，風水能讓居家更為平和，與環境更為和諧。他們相信居家辦公若有好風水能讓人更為放鬆，況且，目前許多中國事物在美國都特別受到歡迎。

風水對任何人都實用，不妨想想你最常用來讀書的地方─桌子，是不是凌亂不堪，而且四處散落食品包裝、書籍和報紙呢？還是整齊清潔，用筆擺放也井然有序呢？雖然風水學複雜程度遠甚於此，但不妨從整齊的書桌做起，有些人覺得在桌面擺設小盆栽或照片也有所幫助，何不現在就安排一下你的工作場所，以風水的角度來提升你的工作效率呢？

Unit 23

隨著飼養寵物的人日益增多，許多公司也在世界各地成立，以提供全面的寵物服務。事實上寵物服務公司成長相當迅速，以致於許多國家視為重要刺激經濟的因素。

單就美國而言，就約有 6 千萬的養狗人士。畢竟，狗稱得上人類最好的朋友，飼主想要給牠們最好的也是再自然不過了。已有幾家頂級的寵物公司成立，像是「犬牙烘培坊」和「三隻狗麵包店」等，為的就是要滿足這些人的需要。這些公司屬於一次購足的店家，提供高品質的狗食、寵物的梳洗設備。

一般的寵物店只販售寵物的基本物品，例如玩具和飼料；相反的，有些餐館的設計，則是要提供狗狗完整的進食經驗。舉例來說，「再吃一口寵物餐館」不只販售寵物的用品和配件，更提供了空調環境、豪華座椅，以及讓狗狗奔跑的寬敞空間，此外還安排狗狗的婚禮和生日派對。

「三隻狗麵包店」將寵物照護提昇到另一個境界─成立了「葛瑞希基金會」。基金會的功能就好比狗狗界的紅十字會，回應苦難狗狗的緊急需求，提供牠們食物、醫療看護與基金。

寵物照護不管在中國、法國和美國等國家，都是一項成長中的行業，因此許多新興公司陸續成立，以滿足飼主的需求，這些公司獨特之處在於將寵物看成客戶，將牠們當成貴族般呵護。

Unit 24

每天早晨六點半的印度孟買，有一群上百人的團體齊聚在臨近的公園運動。男女皆有，老少不一，健康程度也不同；身處印度，你可能以為這是個瑜珈團體，或以為他們要一起慢跑或練習有氧運動，事實上，這其實是個「歡笑俱樂部」。

歡笑俱樂部始於 1995 年，自從那時候開始也傳播到印度其他地區，以及全球四十餘國。合格的歡笑指導老師可以引導活動進行，通常是以深呼吸和伸展運動為開場。接著參與活動的人圍成一圈，嘗試不同的笑法，像是邊跳舞邊笑、發自內心大笑或咯咯大笑等。每一次集會歷時約 20 至 30 分鐘。

你可能認為必須看一部好笑的電影或是聽到笑話才會大笑，其實並不盡然。僅僅聽到別人笑聲也足以引人發笑，而且笑得愈多，更覺得快樂。在歡笑時，就忘卻了痛苦、恐懼、生氣或無聊。部分人士就認為，讓世上每個人每天都大笑，是促成世界和平很重要的一步。

　　歡笑很棒的一點在於它是沒有限制的。參與者可以是任何年紀，他們也不須專門的服裝或裝備。無論男女，或各行各業之人都能加入，包括醫生、經理、工人或是叫賣的小販。甚至來自不同國家，說著不同語言的人也能參與，因為笑是全人類都了解的語言。最棒的是參與者不必很富有。歡笑是不用花錢的！

　　許多公司目前都已為員工開設歡笑俱樂部，因可減壓並提升產值。歡笑俱樂部的成員表示，歡笑讓他們覺得活力再現、身心放鬆且恢復生氣。有了這些個結果，我們都能開懷大笑了！

Unit 25

　　在美國或加拿大的任何一座大都市中，你都可以找到很多各國風味的餐廳。這是因為在大都市中，有許多外國移民開的餐廳，而且美國人喜歡異國食物。這些餐廳呈現出各式各樣烹調的風格及料理。舉例來說，在舊金山你就可以找到法國、義大利、中國、墨西哥菜、日本及越南菜的餐廳。

　　各國風味的餐廳會受歡迎是因為幾個原因：首先，有某些餐廳非常高級，像是法式及義式餐廳。很多家庭遇重要喜慶會在高雅的法式或義式餐廳用餐，在套餐當中可能會有很多道菜。此外，有一些外國的食物也蠻便宜的。很多墨西哥及中式餐廳以實惠的價格提供豐盛的餐點。最後，有些異國風味的食物是有益健康的。例如日式餐廳提供烹調不油膩的新鮮魚類及蔬菜。

　　所以，如果你住在北美的都市裡，你可以一個晚上在伊朗菜的餐廳用餐，另一晚在墨西哥式的餐廳吃飯。你可以享用異國風情的菜餚，並且了解來自世界各地的美食。

Unit 26

　　太平洋樂園之旅帶我們到位於美國西岸的加州，還有太平洋的夏威夷島。美麗的鄉野風光、充滿驚奇的都市、酷斃了的沙灘，這趟旅程擁有每一樣東西！我們首站來到了舊金山。這座城市以它的電纜車聞名，而且人們也的確需要這些電纜車，因為舊金山的地勢起伏很大，還有一些十分陡峭的道路。在海邊，漁船旁有鮮魚店。在這裡，我們一邊享用新鮮的魚，一邊欣賞街頭表演和音樂家的演奏。有一件事是我們絕對不會忘記的，就是宏偉壯麗的金門大橋。

　　旅程中的第二站來到洛杉磯。這是一座充滿刺激並且有許多著名景點的都市。附近的海濱是一片綿延的沙灘。我們參觀了拍攝過「海灘遊龍」的沙灘。我們也去了迪士尼樂園，在那邊我們和米老鼠握手。之後我們被帶到了好萊塢，去看那些主演了一堆片子、賺了一大堆錢的演員所住的豪宅。

　　我們在加州參觀的最後一個地方是聖地牙哥，一個充滿陽光、沙灘、海水和各項水上運動的城市。我們還去了聖地牙哥動物園，它是世界上最大的動物園之一。

　　最後一站我們來到了夏威夷。那簡直是人間仙境！我們坐在有綠色棕櫚樹點綴的金黃色的沙灘上，觀賞令人驚嘆的日落美景。我們也在海洋生物公園看到了色彩繽紛的魚類，然後還去恐龍灣浮潛。晚上則在熱鬧的俱樂部、酒吧和冰淇淋店消磨時光。最棒的事就是我們一邊吃著夏威夷美食，一邊看當地人表演傳統的玻里尼西亞舞蹈。

　　這個假期真是有夠炫。所以當你有空閒時，就搭上飛往美國西岸的第一班飛機，去享受一下人生吧。

Unit 27

　　就像大家一樣，我有很多的人生目標。其中最重要的兩個，就是受完整的教育，和留給後代一個健康的地球。

　　首先，我想要的教育不只是能讓我有能力去獲得待遇好且值得的工作，而且也可以幫我過著令人滿意的生活。我需要一份好工作來養家活口；也許有一天我可以買幢房子。但我也想要去接受通識教育。例如，我想要修文學及藝術的課來豐富我的休閒時光。我要修歷史的課程，藉以了解我們人類是從哪裡來的，將來又要朝哪裡去。

對我來說保護環境也是重要的。我有一份責任去愛護我們的地球，至少保持像我最初看到她的時候一樣。我認為我們應該像那些美國原住民一樣，他們的宗教要求他們去想一想，他們現在的所作所為會如何地影響將來的子孫。我所能做的小小貢獻就是控制我家的人口，以免成為人口成長爆炸的幫兇。我也可以投票給那些放眼未來而不是只為了選舉的候選人。

沒有人願意生活在貧窮之中，但不一定代表我們要有錢才會快樂，特別是教育已為我們準備好充實生活的遠景。同時，如果我們留給我們的子孫一個不健康的地球，我們也不會快樂的。

Unit 28

春暖花開，到哪裡度週末呢？如果你選擇泡溫泉或賞櫻花，都可能躲不掉擁擠的人群。何不來到台東縣關山，享受結合運動和觀光的單車之旅呢？

自行車道環繞著關山鎮長達 12 公里。大部分的車道沿著卑南溪、紅石溪及關山大圳。沿途有水聲以及美麗的水景相伴。

一路前進，景色也隨之改變。沿途八公里，有處綿延無際的稻田風光。潺潺流水，微風輕拂，令人心曠神怡，彷彿置身在米勒的畫中。在小溪旁，你可以看到竹林隨風搖曳，竹葉不經意地飄落水面，隨波漂流。

再往前走，你將體驗到蜿蜒的車道穿梭於滿園的落英繽紛之中，可以聽到車輪踩著落葉的窸窣聲和林中的鳥叫聲。車道近終點處，你或許會與一大片油菜花田，不期而遇成千上萬朵金黃色的花搖頭晃腦，在微風中搖曳。下車來，在金黃色的油菜花田中拍張照片。這照片將記錄下關山鎮單車之旅帶給你的歡愉吧！

Unit 29

競爭，長久以來在不同領域裡一直是進步背後的驅力，例如世界貿易及運動表現。然而，有很多看法是反對人們想成為第一名的慾望。就像一個叫伯納杭特的英國記者所說：「勝利就像毒品一樣。你一旦試過它，就不能沒有它。」

競爭的主要壞處就是它會助長欺瞞之風。每年很多運動員因為服用禁藥來提昇他們的表現，而被判剝奪比賽的資格，可為殷鑑。政客也一直以愛說謊聞名，尤其是在他們很想贏得選舉時，便會說謊來獲得選票。在產業界，用更便宜的價格來生產更多產品的競爭也是十分激烈，這導致公司會在貧窮的國家開設工廠。在那兒，工廠會要求工時長工資低，來剝削勞工。

另一方面，運動競爭意味著運動員必須要盡最大的努力，這樣看比賽會刺激點。而由於政壇上的競爭，會促使從政者努力對國家做一些看得到的政績以取得選票，最後受惠的是每個人。最後，在產業界的競爭下，會使產品價格更低，這對消費者來說無疑是有益的。

總之，競爭有利也有弊。雖然競爭會導致不誠實及剝削，但它的好處仍多於壞處，而且對我們生活中的許多方面都有積極正面的影響。此外，競爭的精神是永遠與我們同在的，而且不論你如何嘗試也很難加以控制。

Unit 30

親愛的家人，

我希望家裡每個人都健康安好。雖然剛開始遭遇了一些「文化衝擊」，但我現在過得非常好。

起初每件事都很新鮮刺激，可是一旦新鮮感退了，挫折也隨之而來。好些時候，我根本連房門都不想踏出半步，而且只要遇到原本在家都很容易，到這裡卻寸步難行的事情，我就變得脾氣暴躁。但情況已有所改善，我也開始調整了。

課業是另一項挑戰。教授指派了大量的閱讀功課，要完全跟上並不容易。而且要分出事情的先後順序更是格外困難。有時教授要求所有學生對一篇文章瞭解的一清二楚，但有時對於某篇特定文章卻又隻字未提。

另一項挑戰就是要與人相處融洽。那就是這裡的人雖然都很好，但很難知道他們的看法，或者他們在想些什麼。我想融入他們，學習處事之道，但我也不放棄當個臺灣人！班上有些華裔學生，我們在課業上互相幫忙，周末也一起出去玩。

我還去了一個令人驚豔的地方：紐約市，那是個多元種族的城市，有來自幾乎世界各國的移民，因此是一個品嚐美食和購物的好去處。而最讓我興奮的就是，我到了洋基球場觀賞了一場大聯盟的棒球比賽。

我期待見到你們大家！

艾利絲敬上

P.S. 謝謝你們上周末來電！很高興聽到你們的消息。

KEY TO EXERCISES

Unit 1

問答

1. The age of puberty sometimes causes problems, but trying to keep healthy can help cope with the problems.

2. I have a skin problem. My serious acne can ruin my life.

3. Physical health will help me deal with ups and downs of everyday life.

4. I eat the right foods and exercise to help make puberty less difficult.

翻譯

1. made him tired out/exhausted

2. He grew stronger and healthier.

3. feels soft

4. The fruit tastes terrible.

5. When accidents happen, be sure to keep calm.

6. Does the sentence sound correct?

Unit 2

問答

1. People in the U.S. believe some superstitions.

2. People in the Middle Ages believed that black cats were witches in disguise. Black cats have been believed to be evil since then.

3. I believe Friday the thirteenth is an unlucky day.

合併或改寫句子

1. I pay him one million dollars, he will not fix the CD player for me.

2. impossible for me to get to sleep

3. is certain that he will take my advice

4. is difficult for him to tell the difference between them

Unit 3

問答

1. The passage introduces the first store where robots are at work.

2. I often buy drinks from vending machines.

3. We can find many things that we need every day, like food, drinks, household goods, magazines, and cosmetics.

4. I don't like to buy things from RoboShop because nobody says hello to me.

合併句子或改寫句子

1. lay on the grass, looking at the twinkling stars

2. was playing the guitar, pretending not to see me

3. is the man dancing with your sister?

4. invited to the party studied in the same school

翻譯

1. He said goodbye, waving his hand.

2. from door to door, selling his home-made ice cream

3. The little girl sat quietly on the floor, playing with dolls.

4. living next door is a lawyer

5. went out, leaving her daughter alone at home

Unit 4

問答

1. According to the author, Hitchcock's films can bring out strong feelings in the viewers.

2. My least favorite movie is war movies because there is too much violence.

3. The title was *Pearl Harbor*. It was about an overwhelming love and surprise attack on the U.S. armed forces at Pearl Harbor on December 7, 1941. Ben Affleck, Josh Hartnett, and Kate Beckinsale starred it.

合併或改寫句子

1. Not knowing how to react, he kept silent.

2. Fearing that he would be arrested, he tried to escape.

3. Having failed twice, he decided not to try again.

翻譯

1. Being seriously ill, he cancelled his journey to Britain.

2. Getting tired of my complaint about the program, he turned off TV.

3. Not wishing to make her angry, I told her a white lie.

4. Feeling the floor shaking, I rushed out of my room.

Unit 5

問答

1. In the big cities, the problem of homelessness is getting serious and is hard to solve.

2. They are living in the parks and the train stations.

3. Poverty and mental disease caused them to be homeless.

合併句子

1. had he finished his dinner when someone knocked on the door

2. is he an excellent surgeon but he also plays the piano very well

3. does he tell us about his past experience

4. confused was he that he didn't know what to do

翻譯

1. working day and night can he earn enough money

2. have I heard such a sweet voice

3. will I reveal the secret

4. Directly opposite him sat a young girl.

Unit 6

問答

1. Matching-making through Internet is becoming a developing business in today's world.

2. A blind date is a date between a boy and a girl who have not met each other before.

3. Matchmakers arrange marriage for others.

4. People are too busy to get to know someone, and they don't want to have a blind date because they think a blind date involves a high degree of risk.

合併句子

1. which/that stands in the center of the park is a work of art

2. who/that wrote the book is a neighbor of ours

3. , who suffers from Parkinson's disease, has been in a nursery home for 5 years

翻譯

1. He is willing to take care of my cat when I am away.

2. how handsome he was when he was young?

3. The mother saved her baby from the fire at the risk of her life.

Unit 7

問答

1. In the U.S., people are beginning to choose nutritious, healthy food as their favorite.

2. Red meat contains high levels of cholesterol. People realize that it is harmful to health.

3. We need the food because it gives us strength to do physical activities.

4. Bread, cereals, vegetables, and fruits are rich in fiber.

合併句子

1. kidnapped his uncle, which made all his relatives furious

2. saw several women in the park, all of whom were doing some exercise

3. is invited to the tea party is welcome

4. is worth doing is worth doing well

翻譯

1. She passed the test, which made her parents proud of her.

2. where she hid the gold

3. Whoever attends the meeting will be given a present.

4. Whatever is in the show room is priceless.

Unit 8

問答

1. Animals communicate with each other through signals or facial expressions.

2. When it is frightened, he runs away with its tail held upright in the air.

3. It dances in the figure of eight, wriggling and shaking its body.

4. They press their lips together.

合併句子

1. We are uncertain whether he will be present.

2. lay there with his eyes fixed on the ceiling

翻譯

1. She walked away angrily, without a word spoken.

2. Humans tend to express their emotions through their facial expressions.

3. I can't hear you with the train roaring along.

4. if he wants to take Chinese medicine

Unit 9

問答

1. Although sun-tanned skin may be fashionable, the sun's rays can be the cause of skin cancer.

2. Tanned skin became fashionable because tanned skin meant that they were rich people. Only rich people spent a lot of free time in the sun.

3. People realize that the sun's rays are harmful to the skin. They may cause skin cancer. So people today protect their skin from the sun.

4. It is between 10 a.m. and 3 p.m.

5. If I have to stay in the scorching sun, I'll wear a long-sleeved shirt and long pants.

合併或改寫句子

1. This is the place where they store something valuable.

2. like the way that Jane organized the class reunion

3. Tell me the reason why you were absent.

翻譯

1. Heavy rain kept us from taking a hike.

2. Read as much as you can.

3. She walked as fast as possible so that she could catch up with us.

Unit 10

問答

1. The story is about why and how the Titanic tragedy happened.

2. She was considered unsinkable, because even if two of her 16 watertight compartments were flooded, she would still be able to float.

3. Because there were not enough lifeboats, 1,500 people stayed behind and were finally drowned.

改寫句子

1. She was so poor that she couldn't afford a meal.

2. I exercise a lot so that I can keep in shape.

3. surprise, he finished the complicated work on his own

4. She plays not only the piano but also the cello.

翻譯

1. joy, all the passengers survived

2. She was so weak that she couldn't walk any farther/further.

3. He fell asleep while he was listening to music.

Unit 11

問答

1. Human bodies have been decorated for different purposes.

2. They dance and sing.

3. Tattoos were used to indicate their social status.

4. The reason might be that they want to show their personalities through tattoos.

改寫句子

1. The more you get together, the more you have in common.

2. The higher you climb, the farther you will see.

3. difficult the job is, I am determined to do it on my own

翻譯

1. The more you read, the more knowledge you will get/acquire.

2. much she eats, she will not get fat

3. "Love" tattooed on his arm

4. you agree or not, he insists on going abroad

Unit 12

合併或改寫句子

1. he lost his right hand, he kept on learning to play basketball

2. You will not finish it in time unless you burn the midnight oil.

3. he found he had no other choice that he faced the music

翻譯

1. how to use cellphone

2. that I should go jogging in the park after school

3. had no sooner arrived at the station than/had hardly arrived at the station when

4. when to go shopping

5. The little boy didn't leave the store until the rain stopped.

Unit 13

問答：

1. People in Tasmania knitted sweaters for penguins to protect them from being killed by oil spills.

2. The oil would make the penguins unable to keep warm and likely to be poisoned.

3. If they are knitted loosely, the penguins' beaks or flippers might be caught in the holes

翻譯：

1. It doesn't matter if/whether; who hurt you; the gift you give to yourself

2. as if he owned the restaurant

3. The earthquake happening; resulted in over 6,000 deaths.

4. although she is sometimes bad-tempered

Unit 14

問答：

1. Four sources. Occupation, location, father's name or characteristic.

2. locational names: D F G J L occupational names: A C I M

3. The characteristic might be brown hair or skin.

翻譯：

1. residents in this region died of; because of having eaten

2. silently paying their

3. plans to gain four pounds in two months, while Joyce wants to lose weight as fast as she can

4. originated from China

Unit 15

問答：

1. It is about what we can see and do in the park and farmland surrounding Chatsworth House.

2. Visitors can watch special animal displays, attend 'Meet the Animals' sessions, and take trail rides.

3. Visitors can join in activities such as Christmas stories, plays and songs inside, while outdoors there are still tractor rides around the farm if the weather is pleasant.

4. We can find a river, small lakes, gardens, and a lot of traditional and modern sculptures.

翻譯：

1. as long as you promise not to stay up all night

2. someone to talk to about their worries

3. Unlike most classmates of mine, I walk to school

4. If the weather is pleasant, we will go to the beach enjoying the warm breeze and the sun.

5. To achieve the goal, we have to work together closely.

Unit 16

問答：

1. Before the 1600's black pepper was uncommon and only the very rich could afford, but now it becomes a spice that nearly everyone in the world takes for granted.

2. Black pepper is native to India.

3. Because the transportation of that time made it difficult for people in Europe to get black pepper.

翻譯：

1. is rumored that Whiney Houston suffers

2. take for granted what our parents have done for us

3. Without your financial support; a complete failure

4. made it possible that people easily traveled from one continent to another

5. These are what you have to do in case of an earthquake

Unit 17

問答：

1. This article is mainly about the cause of sleep deprivation and the problems.

2. There are three aspects: anxiety, school grades/academic achievements, and health.

3. Yes, I find it hard to keep awake in class because I always stay up playing computer games.

改寫句子：

1. The young man makes his own living by designing webpages.

2. There is no doubt that homeworking is a growing trend.

3. Patients have difficulty paying for expensive medical treatments.

翻譯：

1. by learning where our city gets its water; how it is treated

2. There is no doubt that Indian food

3. He has difficulty explaining why

4. Even if you try to escape from reality, the situation is still worsening (getting worse).

5. My grandmother easily dozes off/tends to doze off while watching TV.

Unit 18

問答：

1. ORBIS Taiwan not only offers vision healthcare programs to local people but also supports ORBIS international programs.

2. Because Taiwan has outstanding achievements in ophthalmology and economy.

3. Because in Xinjiang there is strong sunshine, which would damage eyes.

翻譯：

1. your child is not old enough to be home alone

2. Due to rapid growth; require sufficient nutrition

3. not only offers free medical treatment to people; benefits many eye doctors

4. To help people in need; campaign to raise money

5. is best known for its collection

Unit 19

寫作練習：

A: 1. C   2. B

B: 1. The stereo headphones can damage a listener's hearing.

  2. Doing aerobic exercise helps your heart healthier.

Unit 22

寫作練習：

A. 1. CBED   2. CEBDA

B. (1) 1. However   2. For example   3. too   4. But   5. So

  (2) 1. To begin with   2. on the other hand   3. As a result   4. however   5. Finally

    6. On the contrary

漢堡式大考英文段落寫作
Paragraph Writing: Easy as a Hamburger

快速掌握漢堡式英文段落寫作技巧！

林君美 編著

- 囊括所有大考作文題型，從簡函寫作、看圖寫作、圖表寫作到主題寫作，提供豐富的寫作範例及練習題，並有重點分析說明，完全掌握應試技巧。
- 特別提供「評分樣例」，模擬大考作文實際評分方式，並加註評語說明，幫助讀者掌握大考拿分標準，並預估自己的成績。
- 特別講解大考英文作文常見的錯誤，提醒讀者避免錯誤，並附即時練習，進階提升寫作技巧。
- 加碼附贈「寫作練習卷」與「寫作評估表」各一份，並提供兩種配分參考，課堂教學、自我進修皆適用，方便實際練習寫作並評估寫作成果。

跨閱英文

學習不限於書本上的知識，而是「跨」出去，學習帶得走的能力！

跨文化
呈現不同的國家或文化，進而了解及尊重多元文化。

跨世代
橫跨時間軸，經歷不同的世代，見證其發展里程碑。

跨領域
整合兩個或兩個以上領域之間的知識，拓展知識領域。

王信雲 編著
車畇庭 審定

1. **以新課綱的核心素養為主軸**
   網羅3大面向──「跨文化」、「跨世代」、「跨領域」，共24篇文章，引發你對各項議題的好奇。包含多元文化、家庭、生涯規劃、科技、資訊、性別平等、生命、閱讀素養、戶外、環境、海洋、防災等之多項重要議題，開拓多元領域的視野！

2. **跨出一板一眼的作答舒適圈**
   以循序漸進的實戰演練，搭配全彩的圖像設計，引導學生跳脫形式學習，練出「混合題型」新手感，並更進一步利用「進階練習」的訓練，達到整合知識和活用英文的能力。最後搭配「延伸活動」，讓你在各式各樣的活動中FUN學英文！

3. **隨書附贈活動式設計解析本**
   自學教學兩相宜，方便你完整對照中譯，有效理解文章，並有詳細的試題解析，讓你擊破各個答題關卡，從容應試每一關！

獨家克漏字&寫作雙效題本，
從單字句型到作文一路稱霸！
從「引導」到「自由發揮」英文寫作，
本書無所不能！

- 以克漏字題型為主軸提供30篇短文，前18回提供重要句式分析與句型練習；後12回進階教學寫作要點。由淺入深一次學好大考克漏字與非選題。

- 克漏字逐題解析，幫助完整理解短文意旨，釐清文法觀念。

- 特別針對短文設計開放式問答題，深入探討文章意涵並刺激寫作脈絡思考。

- 附解析本，含全文中譯及句型練習解答。

題本與解析本不分售
012-80398G